LOOTIE'S WORLD RUN

MASCOT BOOKS
an imprint of Amplify Publishing Group

www.mascotbooks.com

Lootie's World Run: The Extraordinary True Story of the Fastest Woman to Have Run Around the World

For more information, please contact:
Mascot Books, an imprint of Amplify Publishing Group
620 Herndon Parkway, Suite 220
Herndon, VA 20170
info@mascotbooks.com

Library of Congress Control Number: 2025904320
CPSIA Code: PRV0325A
ISBN-13: 979-8-89138-554-2

Printed in the United States

To James

LOOTIE'S WORLD RUN

The Extraordinary True Story of the Fastest Woman to Have Run Around the World

MARIE "LOOTIE" LEAUTEY

MASCOT® BOOKS
an imprint of Amplify Publishing Group

CONTENTS

FOREWORD xi

1
MARATHON 1

2
NOMAD 7

3
FROM DREAM TO REALITY 13

4
AND SO THE JOURNEY BEGINS 25

5
FREEDOM IN EUROPE 33

6
PANDEMIC 43

7
A SCORCHING SUMMER 47

8
TRACING MY ROUTE BETWEEN LOCKDOWNS 59

9
VILLA VETTA 67

10
ITALIAN SHENANIGANS 73

11
ISTANBUL, AT LAST! 81

12
NORTH AMERICA,
INTO THE UNKNOWN 87

13
MONTANA ADVENTURES 97

14
A FEW WORDS ABOUT BOB 107

15
THROUGH THE GREAT PLAINS 113

16
ACROSS THE RUST BELT 121

17
NEW YORK,
SECOND CONTINENT CROSSED 129

18
IN COMES JAMES 135

19
SOUTH AMERICA,
TWO ON THE ROAD 143

20
THE ANDES 153

21
¡ARRIBA BUENOS AIRES! 161

22
THE BODY 171

23
LAST CONTINENT, AUSTRALIA 179

24
NULLARBOR WILDERNESS 187

25
OZ COUNTRYSIDE 195

26
SYDNEY, THE JOURNEY ENDS 203

EPILOGUE 213
MY WORLD RUN IN NUMBERS 217
ACKNOWLEDGEMENTS 219

FOREWORD

I was invited to write a short foreword, but truly, the book speaks for itself. This is a running book, a travel book rich in geography and history of people everywhere, and so full of humor and stories. It is a fabulous, monumental read—a work of compassion, beauty, and so much more!

Marie "Lootie" Leautey finally ran into the annals of human history on September 1, 2022, in Auckland, becoming the fastest woman ever to run around the world, in 825 days. She is the first woman to run across four continents, covering an incredible 40.5 kilometers per day. The total run of 28,249 kilometers. It is a testament to the mental and physical endurance of Lootie—and to the wonderful World Runners Association (WRA), and everyone who helped her. And to her common-sense attitude in having kept herself free from injury throughout.

A big highlight for me was when Marie came to see me with her partner, James, this spring, and we were able to exchange traveler's tales and hear much more about it all.

And there is so much more!

I hope this book goes from strength to strength and becomes a success!

Rosie Swale-Pope, MBE
1st woman to have run around the world
September 2024

Inner Seas
North Sea
Danmark
United Kingdom
Ireland
Nederland
Deutschland
Česko
Österreich
Italia
Andorra
Balearic Sea
START
Cabo Da Roca
Dec 06, 2019
España
Mediterranean Sea
Gibraltar
Malta
Republika Tunis
Fas
Algérie
Libia
Western Sahara

EUROPE CROSSING
• 15,420 km
• 383 run days
• 40,3 km / run day
• 63 rest days (1 a week)
Eesti
Latvija
Lietuva
A' Bhealaruis
An Ucràin
Moldova
România
Bolgarija
FINISH
Istanbul
Jun 24, 2021
Black Sea
A' Chairtbheil
Caspian Sea
Airmeinia
Türkiye
Chipre
Siria
Leabanon
Ioràc
Ioràn
Iisrael
Coweit
Aegyptus
Bachrain
Arab Saudi

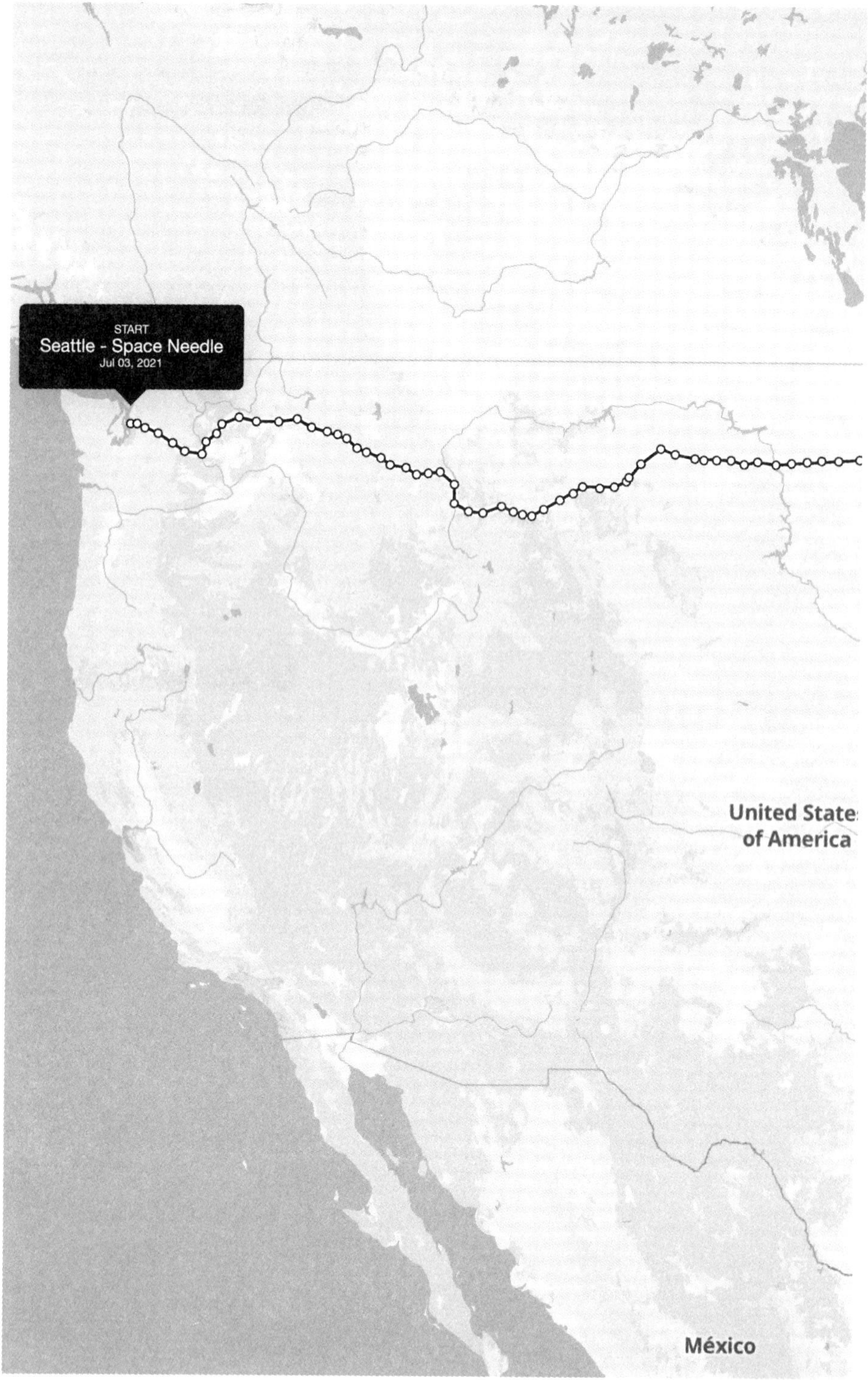

START
Seattle - Space Needle
Jul 03, 2021
United States
of America
México

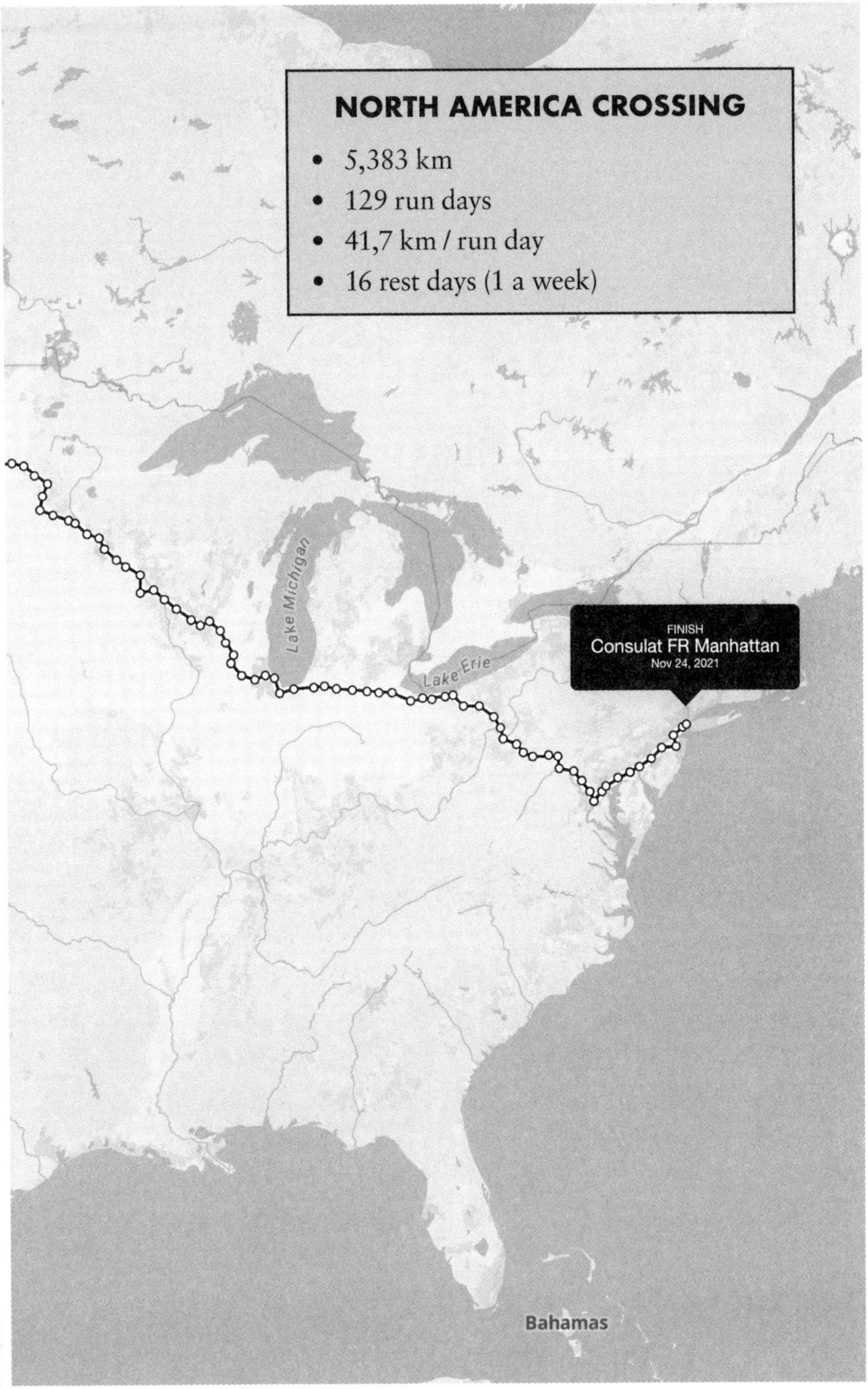
NORTH AMERICA CROSSING
• 5,383 km
• 129 run days
• 41,7 km / run day
• 16 rest days (1 a week)
Lake Michigan
Lake Erie
FINISH
Consulat FR Manhattan
Nov 24, 2021
Bahamas

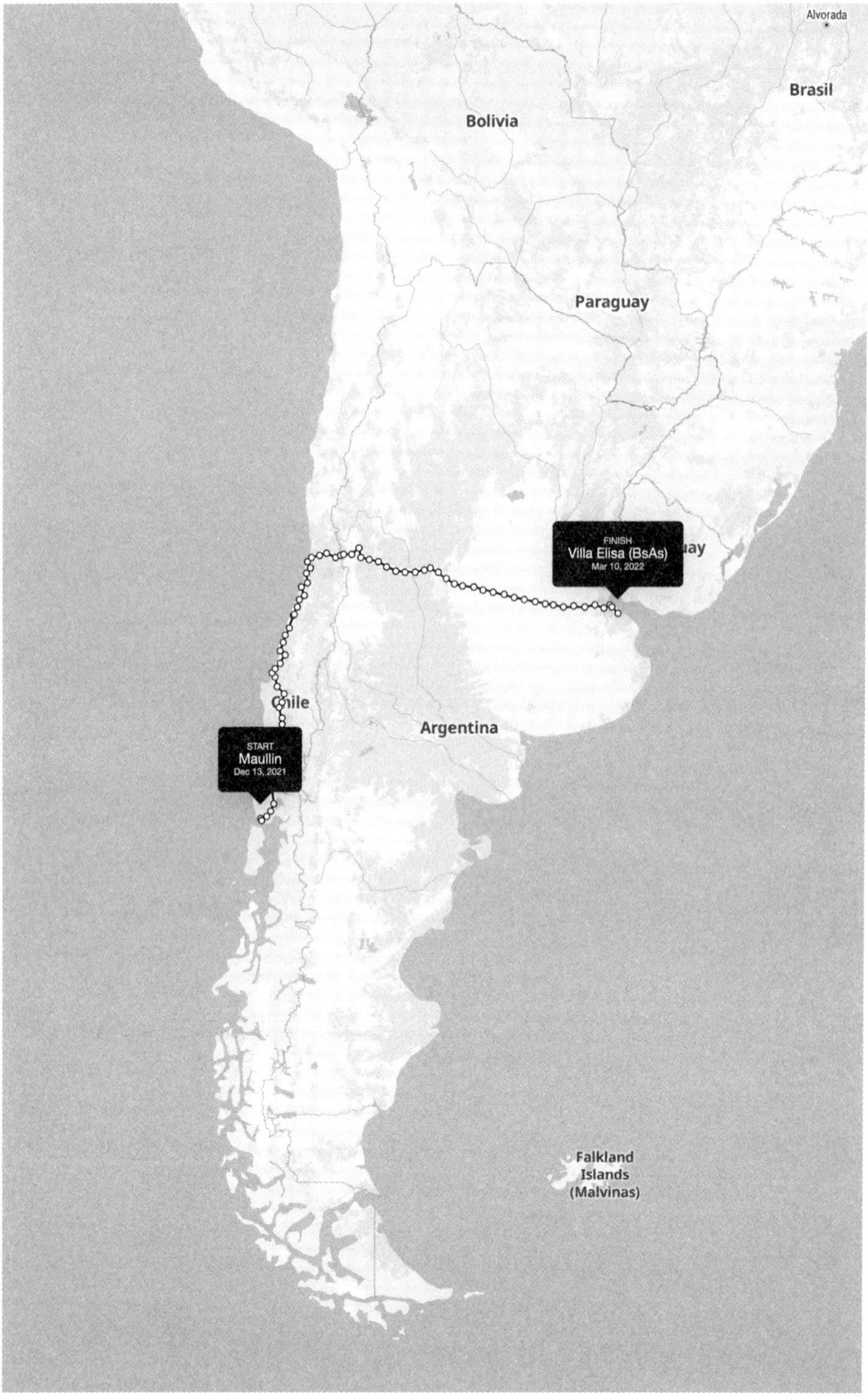
Alvorada
Brasil
Bolivia
Paraguay
FINISH
Villa Elisa (BsAs)
Mar 10, 2022
Chile
Argentina
START
Maullin
Dec 13, 2021
Falkland
Islands
(Malvinas)

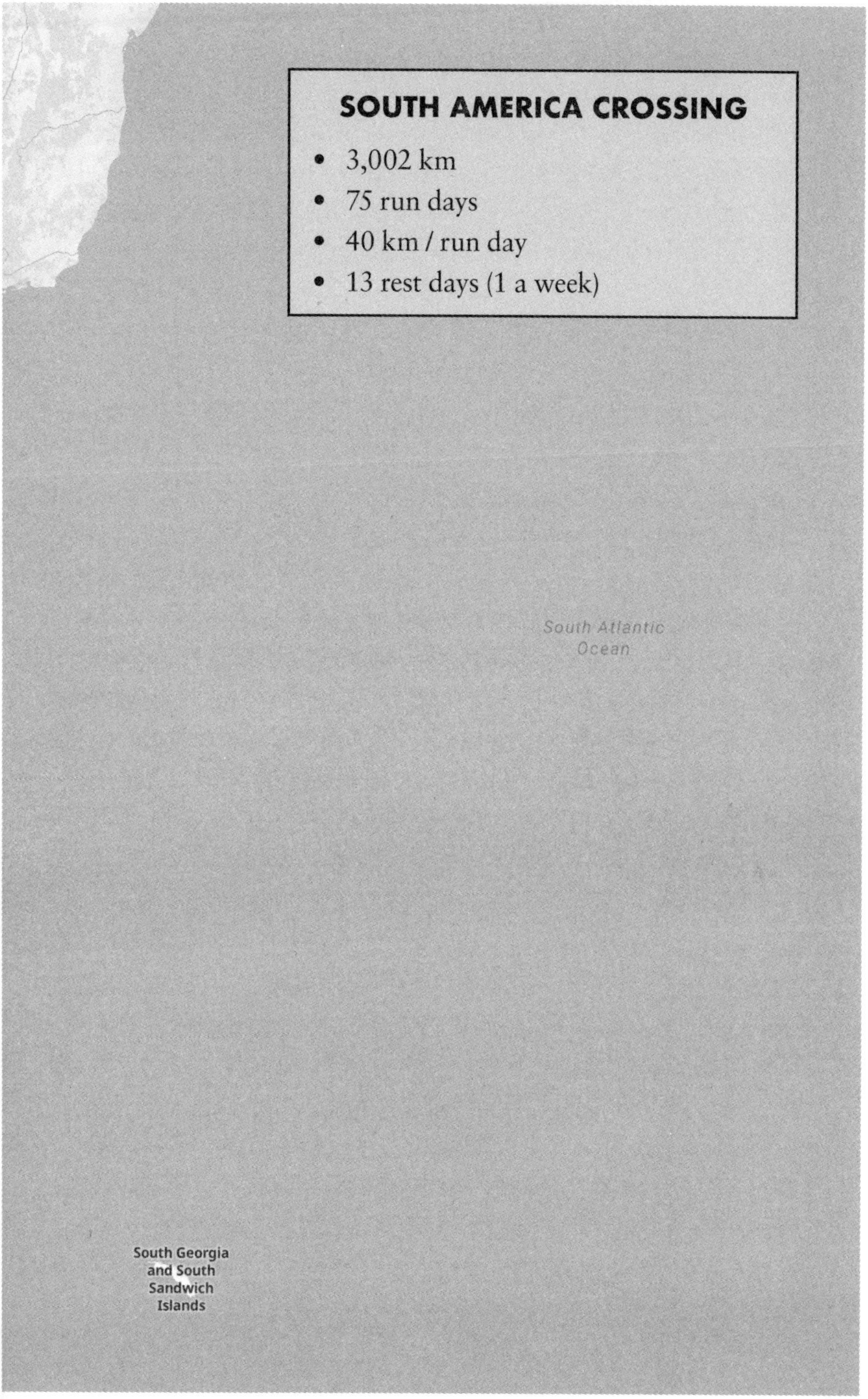
SOUTH AMERICA CROSSING
• 3,002 km
• 75 run days
• 40 km / run day
• 13 rest days (1 a week)
South Atlantic Ocean
South Georgia and South Sandwich Islands

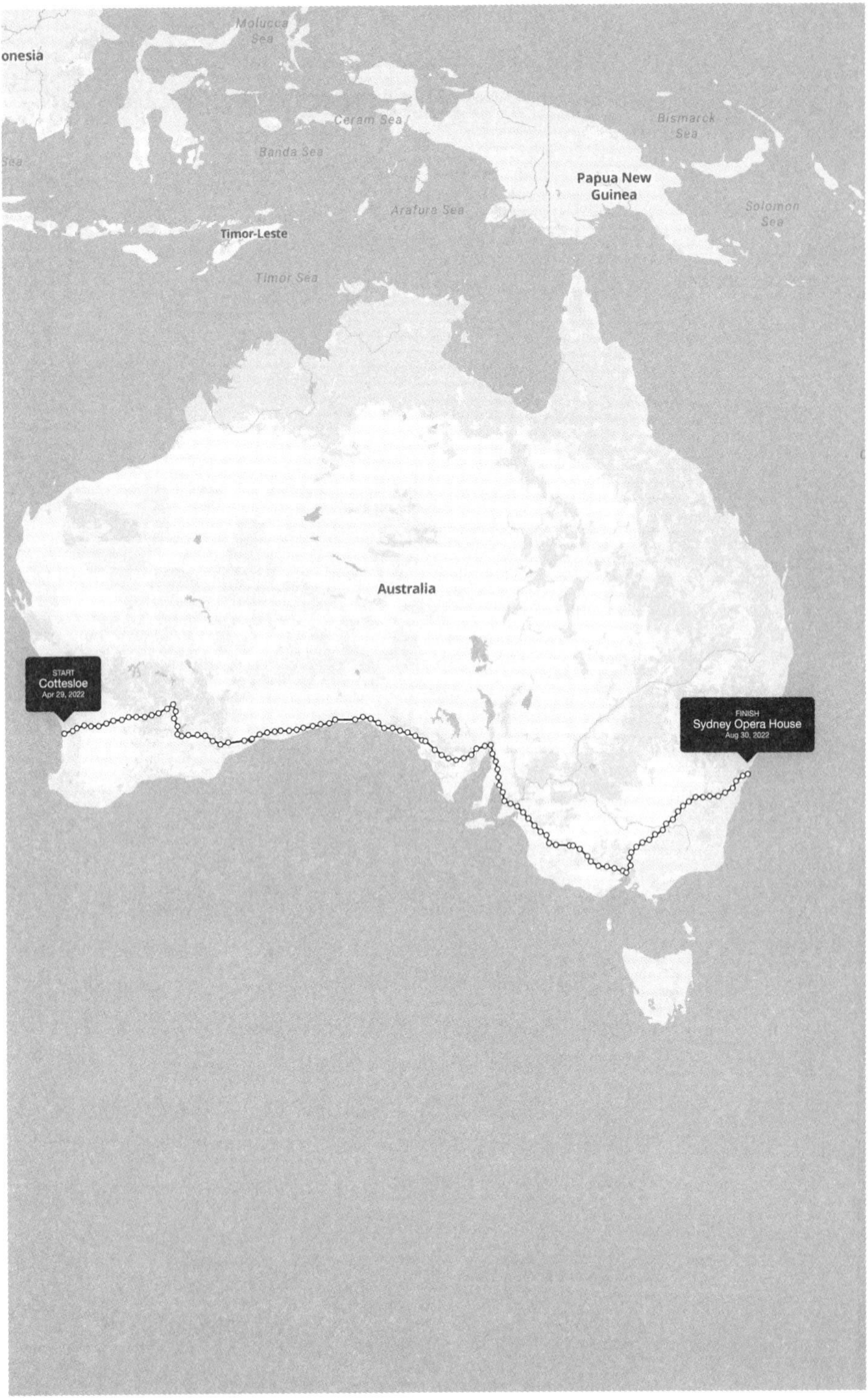
Molucca Sea
Ceram Sea
Banda Sea
Bismarck Sea
Papua New Guinea
Arafura Sea
Solomon Sea
Timor-Leste
Timor Sea
Australia
START
Cottesloe
Apr 29, 2022
FINISH
Sydney Opera House
Aug 30, 2022

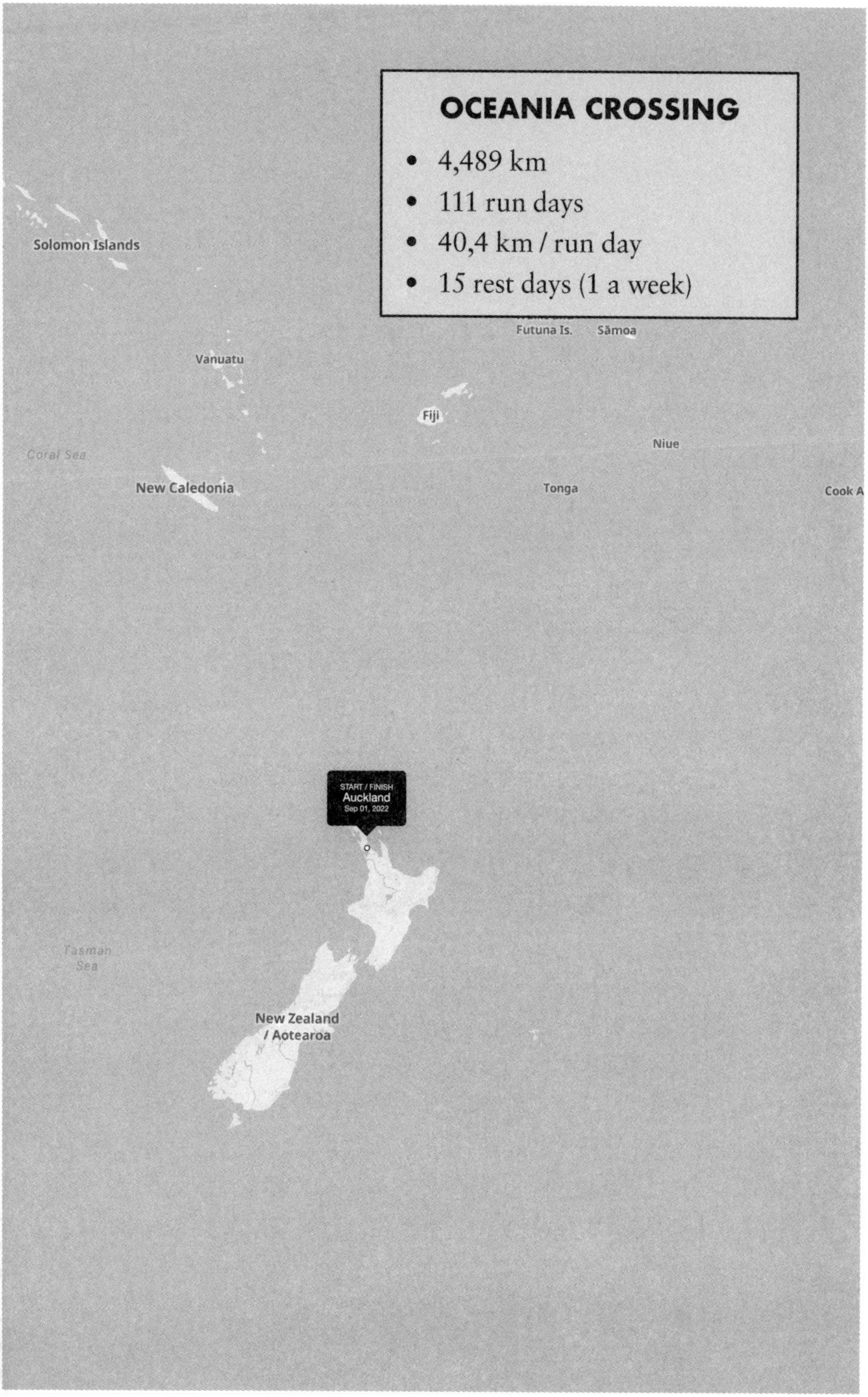
OCEANIA CROSSING
• 4,489 km
• 111 run days
• 40,4 km / run day
• 15 rest days (1 a week)
Solomon Islands
Futuna Is.
Sāmoa
Vanuatu
Fiji
Coral Sea
Niue
New Caledonia
Tonga
START / FINISH
Auckland
Sep 01, 2022
Tasman Sea
New Zealand / Aotearoa

1

MARATHON

Beads of sweat trickle into my eyes as I squint into the distance at the dry spur of land, snaking its way into the blue Aegean Sea. The Greeks' finest hour. My thoughts wander. It was here, in Marathon, that the outnumbered Athenians charged on foot towards the Persian fleet at anchor to achieve a famous victory. It is also from this point that Philippides ran towards the capital city, Athens, to announce the Greek army's victory. A distance that will be forever remembered simply as "the marathon."

I light another cigarette and sip on my warm beer, feeling suddenly uncomfortable and out of place on this trendy beach with its blaring pop music, lying in the sun surrounded by equally lazy people. Something is amiss and evokes a form of sadness in me. I am twenty-six years old. I have just left Edinburgh to take on a job assignment in Athens. I smoke a pack of cigarettes a day and am slightly overweight. My life essentially revolves around the need to build my social network in this new country, learn the language, tackle my new professional mission, partake in cultural activities, and entertain myself at parties. Physically, I have drifted quite far from the hyperactive and sporty teenager I once was. My body had fallen asleep, I reflected uneasily.

My new friend Lisa interrupts my thoughts, “Lootie, do you fancy signing up for a windsurfing lesson with me?”

I ponder for a short while, looking out at the general tranquility of the sea. Why not? I put out my cigarette and, with a sudden invigoration, get up from my sun lounger.

At first, I spend a lot more time in the water than on the board, but something in me awakens. I immediately find something enticingly magnetic in this sport. By taking me away from the noise of the beach, it isolates me and, offshore, reconnects me with sensations that I had long forgotten. The feeling of being in the open air, the salt on my skin, the wind in my hair, my sail filling, and my board slicing through the water. I am independent, alone at sea, and surrounded by nature. It’s seductively simple, and I am hooked.

My job is located on Marathon Avenue, about twenty kilometers away from the beach, and I start a habit of going there every day. I leave the office at the end of my working hours for this peculiar appointment with my newfound freedom. I feel alive again, as if I have rediscovered an essential element of my being. Every afternoon, I show up at the beach and observe the conditions. Wind, or no wind. Surf, or no surf. I often find myself alone with Dimitris, the owner of the resort, and Elias, the windsurfing instructor. We talk a little. They are men of few words. They must find me strange, this slightly plump Frenchwoman, fixated on windsurfing, yet one who does not show herself to be particularly good at it. The two friends often end the day with a run in the pine forest along the beach.

Then comes the day when they ask me to join them. They are twice my age, while I am young and in great shape. At least, I believed so. I put on my sneakers, and off I go alongside them. Less than a kilometer later, I'm out of breath, my lungs on fire. Unable to continue, I let them go and catch my breath as best as I can. I walk back to my car, feeling humiliated. Angry. How did I get to this point? My reaction is commensurate with this monumental disappointment.

That same evening, I throw away what is left of my cigarettes and decide to put my life in order. For the next two weeks, I don't go to the beach. I come home every evening to run around the neighborhood and vow to be able to last ten, twenty, then thirty minutes. I will go running in the pine forest with Dimitris and Elias. I will show them that I have resources and that I am not that wasted youth incapable of stringing three strides together. It becomes an obsession. I also buy a bike. No more driving to work. From now on, I will cycle twenty kilometers every morning across the Penteli Mountain to reach my office on Marathon Avenue.

Two weeks after my dismal effort to run with Dimitris and Elias, I return to the beach, not telling them about the radical changes I have made. The moment I see them getting ready for the run, I follow suit. In silence, I grit my teeth and do the entire five-kilometer loop at their pace. I never miss a run again. The forty kilometers of round-trip cycling to get to the office and back turns into seventy kilometers on the days I go to the beach. Add to this some windsurfing on windy days, a kayak ride on calm days, and the five-kilometer jog in the pine forest. I am out and exercising every spare minute of my day.

I search for and find myself in the effort. I reconnect with the world, with its sensory universe. I experience it, feeling it through the sand under my soles or my bare feet. I breathe in the scents of Greece, of the pine heightened tenfold by the heat, and the sweet smell of the fig trees. I slip into the sea after every run, letting it cool me down and soothe my muscles. Whether it's raining, windy, or under the often oppressively hot temperature, I am in contact with nature every day, without fail. My body sharpens. The sun burns my cheeks and throws golden flashes into my black hair. My muscles roll under my tanned and firm skin. The world leaves its mark on me. My body and mind are the receptacle for it. I feel fully alive, as if a part of my being had been missing for years and has just been put back in its place.

Ten months later, I am radically transformed. Encouraged by Elias and Dimitris, I set off among some five thousand amateur runners on the Athens Marathon course. No sophisticated stopwatch, no gadgets, energy drinks, gels, or other gimmicks for me. I'm as free as I was running in the pine forest.

At the sound of the whistle, we leave the Marathon stadium in a rush. What a feeling to run along this legendary route. As the kilometers pass, I savor and measure the progress made. The last ten months of metamorphosis rush through my head.

I run with ease in this first race of my life. That is until I spot, by the side of the road, the fortieth-kilometer marker. I glance from side to side and suddenly lose my patience. Where is the finish line? A French runner passes by my side as I let out a string of expletives. He stops and grabs my shoulder. "What is going on?"

I explain my confusion to him. I don't see the finish line. And there I learned that the exact distance of the marathon is not just "a little over 40 kilometers," but very precisely 42 kilometers and 195 meters. Never too late to learn!

We turn onto Konstantinou Avenue, and for the first time, I discover the dazzling white and grandiose marble Olympic Stadium in the center of Athens. Tears come to my eyes. My mission in Greece is coming to an end, and this race, this challenge, this masterful arrival, are like the final fireworks which mark the end of the most transformative episode of my life. After three hours and forty-seven minutes of running, having reached the center of Athens, I have completed my first marathon. To use the words of Philippides, the soldier who traveled the same path 2,494 years before me, "Victory!"

It's not just a physical transformation that I've made. It's my lifestyle that's changing. By giving physical activity a central place in my life, I change my relationship with the world. My mode of travel changes. I understand running as the most beautiful way to get from one point to another.

Running becomes my vector of integration, of connection with others, and with my environment. All these cities I am stationed in for weeks or months, what better way to discover them, to feel them, than on foot, as the sun rises?

2

NOMAD

Since leaving France at the age of twenty, I have traveled the world. This is how I had always wanted to live my life, free to move around as opportunities arise. I first left France for Scotland, where I completed my dual legal and financial studies before joining a brewing company. The day the international division advertised for a position in Greece, I applied. I didn't know what profile they were looking for, but it felt like an exotic destination. I told myself that a young French woman who speaks several languages could easily match their expectations. During the interview, I remained vague about the extent of my knowledge of speaking Greek (ancient Greek at that). I got the job, and all I had to do was appear conversant in the language by the time I arrived in Athens!

My contrasts and boldness are my strengths; they intrigue. My cultural mix, my questions and answers often surprise, just as much as my existence, which fits into two suitcases, always ready to be packed for a new destination. I enjoy this game of discovering myself, and the world, among these new destinations, making a home and a living in any environment. My nomadism is my freedom. A joyous way of life.

Is it to preserve this freedom that I have never moved back to France during my adult life? Is this fear of not being able to flourish in my country of birth irrational? I always had the impression that the outcome would be unsurprising in France. I know what is expected of me; my place seems defined. The university where I studied, my diplomas and my work say something about me. Inevitably, they would lead me to get into established patterns, settle down, buy an apartment, get a mortgage, repay loans, and go on vacations: winter in the mountains and summer in the sun. Abroad, I do not feel this pre-ordained fatalism or, as I see it, the mundane, established model. I am, de facto, outside the norm and do not have to conform.

I grew up in Rouen, the chamber pot of Normandy, as it is often dubbed. Unflattering, the expression refers to the geographical particularity of the city: a basin surrounded by the low hills of Canteleu, Mont-Saint-Aignan and Sainte-Catherine. In the center of this natural enclosure, the River Seine makes its way along filthy and disreputable quays. In the 1990s, the years of my adolescence, that picture was still quite accurate. In Rouen, my gaze staggers wherever I look, not only at the hills, but also at a ready-made future. I suffocate. I miss the horizon, my line of flight.

Of course, Rouen is also the "City of a Hundred Steeples," the "Museum City," where the "Maiden of Orleans" was burned at the stake. The port city does not lack charm, with its mediaeval buildings and cobbled streets. One need only to escape the valley to breathe. Follow the holiday route towards the mountains, with their captivating peaks that pull the gaze and the soul upwards. Up where the pure air burns the lungs, at the bend of each path where my parents made us walk every summer morning to evening. Me, my brothers and sister. I understood it from a young age: the world begins beyond the hills. So, I seize the first opportunity to leave the chamber pot and embark on Erasmus, the European universities exchange program.

This opportunity fills me with such joy that I lose my marbles. I am offered Glasgow, which I ridiculously confuse with Oslo, and accept on the spot. I already imagine myself in Norway, in a wooden cabin with a view of the fjords and life in the great outdoors. What a fool I am! Of course, it turns out to be yet another port city, foggy and industrial. At least it is somewhere else.

In 1998, there is no need to exile yourself to the Antipodes to feel far away. I don't have a cell phone, and none of my friends have an email address. Social networks do not exist. This is still the time of postcards and handwritten letters. I am in unfamiliar territory, pushed out of my comfort zone, and the game consists of reaching out to others without fear of appearing too different, since as a foreigner I am different anyway. I have the extraordinary feeling that everything is beginning.

In my first year in Glasgow, I complete my degree while working shifts in a bar to earn a little money. The thick Scottish accent of the local customers is so hard to understand that I am assigned to just clearing tables. It feels like I have to prove all my worth, starting from scratch. I can't hold a conversation or crack a joke. Within a year, my ear has become accustomed enough. I end up in my first adult job teaching law at the university, dispensing lectures and seminars. I rejoice at having established myself and finding myself in a decent situation in a country that was foreign to me not so long ago.

I enjoy the incredible sense of satisfaction of having made it through my endeavors. But I soon discover that teaching is not for me. I need a job that is more hands-on and action-oriented, allowing me to travel. I take on a position in the neighboring city of Edinburgh in the finance department of a brewing company that is expanding internationally.

At twenty-eight, I established myself in Scotland for a few years, embarking on long work assignments in Greece and Germany. I decide to push the nomadism cursor even further by taking a 100 percent travel job for a major soda brand. Spending an average time of two months per country, I wander from head office to factories and warehouses, traveling from hotels to airports with my two suitcases in tow. My assignments take me through many countries across Central and Southern Europe, and as far as Nigeria and Siberia. I measure my luck, being able to settle shortly in these countries, explore their capitals, and converse with their people. No other job will satisfy me as much and on all levels as this one. It was also extraordinarily intense, and I kept up the pace for two and a half years. We didn't talk about carbon footprints at the time or the absurdity of hopping on a plane like some people take the metro. I slowed down the pace, allowing myself to settle a little longer in places.

Thirteen years after I ran my first marathon, I am sitting at my office, on the thirtieth floor of a building in the business district overlooking the bay of Singapore. The view is impressive. The Marina Bay Sands hotel dominates the estuary, with its 150-meter-high towers supporting a long boat-shaped terrace lined with palm trees and adorned with an infinity pool. Further down, the Louis

Vuitton pyramid store floats on the water alongside the ArtScience Museum in the shape of a lotus flower and the futuristic Apple store, a floating glass dome under construction. In the distance, gardens dotted with giant luminous trees and, as far as the eye can see, the sea. Its waters are covered with a long line of ships, waiting at the entrance of the second-largest port in the world.

During five years in Singapore, I have had ample time to explore the country in every detail, to savor "the syrup of the streets," one of my grandmother's favorite expressions. Ah yes! The syrup of the streets: the urban theatre, the comings and goings of passersby and shopkeepers, the noise of the city, and the discussions of table neighbors. My grandmother consumed it, sitting on a café terrace for entire afternoons. I have fond memories of the time spent with her in the streets of Paris, taking in the atmosphere and observing the world before me. I acquired the conviction early on that the essence of life was outside, beyond the next hill, held in the curiosity of what lies behind. My syrup is from the world, and I vowed to drink it abundantly.

My assignment as a financial consultant for a large music streaming group is coming to an end. So much the better, because I am getting restless. I listen absentmindedly to the conference call that feels like an eternity. Lost in my thoughts, I scribble in my notebook and blacken the pages with images of the city with futuristic constructions and emerging spheres spread out at my feet. My imagination takes over. I hang up and examine my sketches. One of them astounds me.

The drawing represents a female silhouette standing on a globe. She looks like Mafalda, my favorite childhood cartoon character. A brazen little girl, clinging to her globe that she carries everywhere.

This seven-year-old cheeky girl, created by the cartoonist Quino, is astonishingly mature for her age, and professes her political, humanist, and feminist flights of fancy. I don't know how she found her way into this Singapore on paper, at the tip of my pen. But it is her, the only difference being that she does not carry the world in her hands; she runs around it.

My thoughts are racing. This is the first time I have formulated this idea so precisely. Is it simple serendipity or the expression of an unconscious desire that lies dormant within me? I'm almost forty; maybe I need to shake up my pace a little. Am I at risk of falling asleep in my comfortable position as financial director in Singapore, a country renowned for the quality of life of its expatriates? So, running around the planet? Why not!

Perhaps it is for all these reasons that this sketch of little Mafalda galvanizes me. Looking at it, I'm no longer in my office on the thirtieth floor of Marina Bay; I am drifting away. I imagine the power of the project that is emerging, utopian, yet so real. Promising adventure, discovery, and a daily street syrup to quench my thirst for elsewhere. The effort of the daily runs to intensify the sense of reward of the journey. It's obvious that I have always carried this world run within me. I just did not know it. It is the pinnacle of my nomadic life. My holy grail. All I have to do now is dare.

3

FROM DREAM TO REALITY

The humid air of Singapore engulfs me as I leave the office and walk towards the metro station. Thoughts swirl in my brain in a continuous flow. Has this already been done? Have any men or women attempted this adventure before me? And if so, how did they do it? Later that evening, I set out in search of answers. My research leads me to the World Runners Association (WRA). I discover that there are six people, five men and one woman, who have already run around the globe. This madness is, therefore, possible. Furthermore, there is a regulation which governs the exercise.

The rules are simple and logical, and there are ten of them. I focus on the main ones. Cross a minimum of four continents, from ocean to ocean, and travel a minimum total distance of 26,232 kilometers. The circumference of the earth is 40,000 kilometers, and 70 percent of the planet's surface is covered with water. So, at a constant latitude, the maximum land surface encountered is 26,232 kilometers. One must also pass through two antipodal points (diametrically opposite points on the earth's surface). Run in a continuous direction, and document your run as precisely, transparently, and completely as possible.

Looking at my computer screen, I try to understand and ingest this singular legislation. I'm already on my way. I have dared, dared to imagine that this world run was possible. That I would be able to experience it. Dared to gather information and visualize an itinerary that would take all these rules into account. A mechanism has been triggered that nothing will stop. After my drawing of Mafalda, I have a structure for my dream, and the WRA makes it achievable.

I am not an athlete, yet it seems to me that all my life, I have been preparing for this monumental project. All these years I've spent putting on costumes that weren't quite cut out for me, accepting ambitious missions in cultures different from my own and in languages that weren't always familiar to me. Over the last two decades, how many times have I had this feeling of not having the right profile but still going for it, hopping on a plane with my two suitcases in tow? Over time, I have not only overcome the fear of jumping into the void, but I have also developed a taste for it. The corollary to these leaps of faith is solid discipline, essential to avoiding a painful crash.

I set to work and begin building the bridge between imagination and reality with patience and determination. My modus operandi is based, above all, on organization and planning. I read extensively about the experiences of my six predecessors, and it quickly becomes clear to me that if the outcomes were the same for each, the paths and motivations differed. I will have to chart my trajectory with the WRA framework and the experience of my elders as my only guides. What excitement to start from a blank page!

I start by reading the book, *Just a Little Run Around the World* by Rosie Swale-Pope, the British adventurer who set out for a world run in 2003, solo and unsupported—the first woman to have done so. Her account of the journey is captivating. She followed a Northern Hemisphere route, taking her from her hometown of Tenby, Wales, all the way through Siberia and to Magadan. From there, she hopped across the Bering Strait and ran into the wilderness of the most inhospitable Alaskan territories. Through all kinds of brutal weather and extreme isolation, Rosie's joyful, gripping tale of her 20,000-mile journey enthralls me. Yet, I feel this is not the experience of the world I am seeking for myself.

I then read books by Serge Girard, the French runner. He is a pioneer of the discipline and the 2017 author of the fastest run around the world in 434 days. I send him a message and end up on a phone call with Laure, his wife, who was in charge of logistics for her husband's adventures. Though exciting, the phone call leaves me wanting more. I am not made of the same wood as Serge, an extreme adventurer whose aspirations and performances are worthy of a champion. Ambitious and gifted with a winner's mentality, he was able to attract sponsors who granted him a substantial budget, allowing him to leave with an able crew, vehicles, and support. I do not recognize myself in either this ambition or these resources.

It is upon reading the book *The World at My Feet* by Australian world runner Tom Denniss that I feel I have found something close to my ideal in the same spirit that I envision. Tom set off on the roads of the world with his wife Carmel, who accompanied him by car. They shared a unique and exotic family trip. His approach speaks to me more. I send him an email, and over time, a camaraderie develops between us. Tom is humble and generous enough to respond to all my messages and to always encourage me. He is interested in my preparations and shares with me anecdotes from his adventures. His kindness reflects a form of handing over, and gradually, he gives me the confidence and legitimacy I need.

First, I need to check that my body can support the load of such an expedition. I increase my training volume substantially. My job happens to be about twenty kilometers away from my apartment, and I start running home most evenings. Running home rather than running to work, to avoid time constraints and, therefore, stress. Besides, I don't use a watch. I don't want to impose a pace on myself. I let my body find its rhythm, that of lasting endurance.

I decide that the backbone of my preparation would consist of a series of mini adventures, which I call "marathon trips." These trips aim to replicate the conditions of the world run's autonomy and self-sufficiency, testing my ability to plan, execute the plan, and take pleasure in the achievement.

During my first year of preparation (there will be two), I organize five such trips, ranging from three to eight running days in succession. Singapore being a small island of 120 kilometers in circumference, with an extreme tropical climate, I decide to undertake these runs in neighboring and more temperate Australia. From 2018, all my days of leave are devoted to the sequence of these marathons. No more returns to France for reunions with family or friends. I dedicate myself completely to the project.

Training on the long, unfamiliar roads of Australia allows me to put to test the very concept of the journey that awaits me. I'll be running across the world, self-sufficiently, towards the unknown. Does it provide the sensations and rewards I expect? The answer is immediate. My pleasure in traveling whilst using running as a means of transport is increased tenfold. The feeling of freedom is extraordinary. It disconnects me instantly from normal life. Time is of no essence. I have all day to cover the distance, and there is no pressure of time, pace, or anything else. I let the road, the environment, and the conditions dictate my pace. I can stop for as long as I want to enjoy a particular view or observe and listen to the wildlife, the kangaroos, and parrots. I am free to set up camp wherever I want. I feel the hospitability of nature. Excited by these first experiences, I regularly report to Tom, whom I consider the most qualified to give me a reasonable opinion. I read and reread his book until the pages fall out. I, too, want to experience the exhilaration of discovery, to learn, feel, and share.

During this preparation, I am confronted with a wide range of conditions: wind, rain, cold, and oppressive heat. I accept these elements, even welcome them. I know they will be an integral part of the journey, and why would I complain about them when I have chosen to be outdoors every day?

In Singapore, temperatures are regularly over thirty degrees Celsius, and every day the humidity is above 90 percent. Before each run, I monitor not only the weather but also the pollution index, which spikes when neighboring Malaysia and Indonesia burn their forests for palm groves. Sometimes, I get showered by the monsoon rains. I am ready for anything.

I purchase a big, laminated world map and start tracing itineraries with the tip of my pen. I want to choose a route that looks as close as possible to a true circumnavigation, covering both the

Northern and Southern hemispheres. I decide that the order would be: first, Europe (from Portugal to Turkey), then part of Southeast Asia, Australia, New Zealand, North America, South America, and finally a part of Northern Africa, before heading back to my starting point in Portugal. This plan will allow me to run on all six populated continents and cross four in their entirety. I will run on a West to East direction and also pass by two antipodal points, therefore abiding by all the rules set by the WRA.

To escape the rigors of extremes, I optimize the timing of my journey. At a minimum, it seems essential for me to avoid crossing the Australian desert in the middle of summer and North America or the Andes in the depth of winter. By taking to the road in December in the South of the Old Continent, I should travel without too much risk of suffering the harshness of the seasons.

I spend all my free time developing the details of the plan. I devote most of my lunch breaks and evenings to it. On my screen, I open Google Maps. I move my cursor on the map, simulate routes, and zoom in to check the state of the terrain. I know that the most ambitious projects become possible from the moment you plan them seriously. Using Excel tables, I classify and group all the useful information. On each line, I list the stages, the cities of departure and arrival, the number of kilometers, and the positive elevation. I note the options for supplies and accommodation on arrival, and the type of road (main, secondary, or trails). Seven hundred stages to plan across the continents.

I also need to put my equipment to the test. What do I need? How much does it weigh? Above all, how will I transport my gear? Apart from a few sets of clothes, I will bring as little as possible. I will need a computer to update my itinerary, download my GPS records, and write my daily blog. This is essential not only to share the trip with my loved ones but also to keep a precise recording of it. I need a minimum of two GPS devices to record my runs, as well as a satellite beacon and a handheld, lightweight tracker capable of geolocating me and triggering help if necessary. I decide to use a stroller to carry all my gear (twelve kilos worth of it), because running with such a weight on my shoulders would put me at greater risk of injury.

Of the six previous world runners, four of them were self-sufficient. Rosie Swale-Pope, the British adventurer, pulled a cart, while Jesper Olsen, Tony Mangan, and Kevin Carr pushed a stroller containing their gear and supplies. I decide that pushing would be easier and more intuitive than pulling. It would allow natural momentum to imprint a rhythm. I do a little bit of research to ensure I get a very sturdy model of a stroller, one that can handle the weight and the wide variety of terrains and conditions I will encounter.

I soon realize that I will have to progress in complete self-sufficiency for periods of up to a week. In both the heart of North America and the Australian desert, there are road segments of several hundreds of kilometers without a village or refueling station. I need to find some appropriate camping gear. I first opt for a tree hanging tent model, the interior of which closes tightly, preventing eight-legged species and other crawling horrors from slipping inside. I test it during my marathon trips in Australia. I hang it from the trees like a hammock. After two agonizing nights in suspension, it feels more like a sarcophagus than a haven of rest. I finally chose a classic and inexpensive model, light and versatile. Weight is a crucial consideration, and I am conscious that I will have to push my equipment on each of my runs, on every steep hill and rugged road.

Month after month, the project progresses. There remains a significant consideration. How much will this world run cost me, and how will I finance it? If I add up all the daily and logistical expenses, I arrive at a pretty tidy sum. These include daily accommodation and food costs, equipment replacement (such as shoes), communication costs for mobile and satellite devices, insurance, flights from one continent to another, website setup and maintenance, as well as unknown contingencies. I have always made a point of not depending on anyone and guaranteeing my autonomy, and it seems that I will have to work hard and make sure I can go through this project using my own savings.

In any case, how would I go about looking for sponsors—me, who, on paper, has nothing to accredit my ability to go all the way? I did try to knock on a few doors, on the insistent advice of several friends, without any result. My funniest exchange was undoubtedly the one with the brand of my stroller. I sent a well-written email in which I detailed my adventure in broad terms and highlighted the fact that I chose one of their models specifically for its robustness. I told them that their product was going to travel around the planet and cover more than 26,000 kilometers for the cause of women, a stroller world record in itself!

Their answer was fabulous. In typical American corporate lawyer style, I was told that "the use [I] intend to make of the stroller is not in compliance with the general conditions of use recommended by the equipment manufacturer, and [that they] therefore release themselves from any responsibility linked to this use during my adventure."

Well, the matter was settled! I will bear the financial burden of this trip alone, put all my savings into it, and I hope it will suffice. I am certain I will have no regrets when my pockets are empty, because I know my heart will be full. I now count my savings and expenses in “run days.” A bottle of wine, for example, doesn’t cost twenty dollars. No. It costs a significant portion of a day running around the world! The enormity of this adventure and what it symbolizes for me deserves, in my opinion, this level of sacrifice.

The more I refine my plan, the lighter I feel. This plan is my ship upon which I will sail around the globe. The more robust, intelligent, and adaptable it is, the more it will allow me to appreciate everything that the journey has to offer me. I will just have to take out my butterfly net, catch all the flavors and scents, and let the world leave its mark on me. Free.

To complete this exceptional journey, I need a commitment to match it. I decide to associate with an NGO (nongovernmental organization) focused on women’s rights. I choose Women for Women International (WFWI). It is an organization that helps women affected by wars and conflicts and supports them in the reconstruction of their communities and their quest for leadership and emancipation. For them, I aim to collect at least one euro per kilometer traveled.

At the end of 2018, I complete my longest preparation run, a journey of eight marathons in eight days in a circular loop of more than 320 kilometers around Perth, Australia. I am moving in world-run conditions, with a stroller carrying my equipment and camping gear, all alone on the roads. On Christmas Day, I run on a forty-kilometer straight line, between North Dandalup and Byford. Around me is wild Australia. I see a few ranches, but not a soul, only the immensity of the sun-drenched plains. A car passes by, the only one during the whole morning heading to Byford. About an hour later, the same car comes back towards me. A hundred meters in front of me, it parks on the shoulder. Should I be worried? I am alone on the road. What if I'm in the wrong place at the wrong time, and this guy spotted me with bad intentions on his first pass? I have no escape.

As I run past the car, the window opens. A big man, built like a Viking, turns towards me. His biceps are as thick as my thighs, he's covered in tattoos, and wearing sunglasses. A ZZ Top grey beard flows down his chin, and a huge smile splits his face from ear to ear. The driver hands me a bag of food and two bottles of water, wishes me happy travel, and points out a tree further down the road.

"Do me a favor," he says. "It's Christmas. Go and enjoy these in the shade down there with your baby. The sun is beating hard. It's going to be a long day for you, there's nothing before Byford. Good luck."

I stammer a "thank you," and before I have time to start a conversation and explain to him that there is no child in the stroller, he is already far away.

I understand, in this encounter, that I will have nothing to fear from the road. I have with me a shield made of steel. This stroller will be my greatest ally, since in the eyes of passersby, I am a woman who goes jogging with her baby. I understand that the existence of a universal taboo, which protects the mother and her child, will be my protection against any possible bad encounter.

At the beginning of 2019, returning from this marathon trip, I email Tom. I give him my impressions and write a summary as a reminder of all the training I carried out since the start of my preparations. His answer comes back shortly after. He congratulates me and writes, "If you can run these marathons like you have done so far, you are capable of running around the world."

It's Tom who says it. I'm ready! I exult.

4

AND SO THE JOURNEY BEGINS

It's dawn, December 6, 2019. I haven't slept much, but I feel energized and in great shape. I have been thinking about this day for two years, the big departure. I have never been so ready in my life. A unique journey is about to begin, where everything must be invented, including my morning routine. I take a shower, eat a few cookies mechanically, and watch the minutes tick by. I am eager to get going. I resist the urge to open my bag again. Last night, I shed a few kilos of excess weight, and I'm sure I could have lightened it even more. I check the pressure of the wheels on my stroller and pack the "Women for Women" flag in the pocket of my jacket. I repeat the same gestures and the same checks, over and over again. I'm waiting for my parents to get ready, as they are coming to see me leave. Let it begin, damn it!

At Cabo da Roca, on the West Coast of Portugal, the sun is just starting to light up the horizon. The red tip of the lighthouse stands out brightly against the dark blue sky. At the foot of the building, a stele indicates that here is the westernmost point of Continental Europe. On it, a quote from Portuguese poet Luis de Camões is engraved, "The place where the land stops and the sea begins."

For me, though, it's the opposite. The land begins here and extends to the Bosphorus, the banks of which will mark the end of my first continental crossing. What does the adventure to Istanbul have in store for me? I explore the small, deserted place on the edge of the cliff, 150 meters above the ocean. Isolated, dramatic, and wild, the place is an invitation for contemplation.

But it's cold out here, and I'm starting to shiver. Time to get active and hit the road! My parents take the first photos of this journey. I pose in my pink T-shirt, hair blowing in the wind and the Atlantic in the background. That's it. If all goes well, I'm off for over two years of daily marathon runs and a unique experience of the world.

What could be going through their minds at this moment? They came to visit me in Singapore and embraced my project with enthusiasm, realizing through our discussions, how serious I was about it. Throughout these two years of preparation, they have never shown the slightest surprise or concern. Cautious not to upset my plans, they waited until the last minute before offering to accompany me to Portugal. Their discretion and normalizing attitude helped me to focus on the serenity of my journey. But that's not to say they were indifferent! What parents would be indifferent to the idea of letting one of their children set off alone on the roads of the world?

Deep down, I wonder what they think about all this. Does my trip awaken in them an unfulfilled desire for adventure? Does it make them dream, too? I think about it. As a former marathon runner, my father took refuge in training and the occasional race to escape from an intense professional and personal life. My mother also ran until a back injury shattered her ambitions as a marathon runner. With this adventure, I start a journey that they could never have afforded or even imagined. I'm reading between the lines, but this morning, I feel that my step into the unknown connects with them. Is it pride, worry, lost opportunities, or perhaps a mixture of all three?

Thoughts jostle in my mind in a continuous flow of emotions, pangs in the heart and bursts of happiness. I have the feeling that I have just torn my jacket, my T-shirt, and my rib cage. I am opening myself to the wind and the elements. An intense feeling of freedom of a magnitude I have never known before, invades me. I have dared, I have put everything on the line, and I am giving myself entirely to this journey. At forty-two years old, a petite woman of 1.64 meters, here I am, at the edge of the Atlantic Ocean, with the whole world in front of me, and feeling oh, so small. The exhilaration of these first strides is magical; all the extravagance of this adventure dawns on me in powerful reminders. I already know that this is the best thing I have done in my life.

Now that I am on my way, I also have to honor the first appointment of my journey. My family has agreed to all meet me for Christmas in Sevilla. It's been years since we spent a holiday together, and the world run has given us all an occasion to gather. There will be my parents, my two brothers, my sister, their spouses, and my six nephews and nieces. According to the route plan, I will reach the Andalusian capital in three weeks. This deadline, so close to departure, puts a bit of early pressure on me.

What a monumental shame it would be for me to fail before their eyes, so early in the adventure! I do have some pride! Between these little moments of doubt, I take time to appreciate my first day of running, the crispness of the air on my skin and in my lungs, the scent of eucalyptus, the views of the ocean and the sound of the surf, the sand crunching beneath my soles, and the ballet of surfers dancing on the waves. I am running this inaugural marathon almost exclusively by the sea.

I stop off in Lisbon at the end of day one. In the evening, fed and rested, I leave the hotel to stretch my legs and head towards the famous Torre de Belém. Along the way, smartphone in hand, I photograph the typical façades of the Portuguese capital, the laundry drying at the balconies. I stroll through the gardens leading to the tower, as the chords of a guitar resonate in the crowded paths. I am not the only one who wants to visit the place. Among the onlookers, I watch the setting sun sublimate the Torre de Belém with touches of orange, pink, and purple. While I'm recording a video for my friends, the guitarist plays "Stand by Me." Everything is so beautiful, magical—it's like a scene from a movie.

I let myself be consumed by this fabulous journey. I feel I already belong to the road, to the random encounters I meet, and landscapes that I cross. My body is ready to put in the miles. I don't feel any particular fatigue. It's so much easier to run here, in this climate, than in Singapore, where the heat and humidity are crushing. Every day, I see the trace of my satellite beacon put a little more distance between Cabo da Roca and my updated position. I make it a point to write my online blog after each run. For me, above all, so I won't forget anything about this exceptional adventure. But also, for my family and my friends, to share with them the richness of each day, my discoveries, and emotions. Every day, I publish a report, accompanied by a photo gallery of the day, the map, and links to the Garmin and Strava accounts, where my GPS trace is recorded in detail.

From the start, this trip offers me a new relationship with time. Like most of us, my private and professional lives have always been marked by constraints and deadlines. From now on, I don't have to answer to anyone. The only measurement that matters is mileage, the slow progress on the route I have planned, and the rhythm of my strides. Time loses all its value. What a luxury to escape its dictatorship for a few years!

I leave every morning at dawn, and I have no pressure. No one is waiting for me anywhere. At the start of my trip, my appointment in Seville for Christmas constitutes the only obstacle to my total freedom.

I run through the countryside of Portugal, heading inland and south toward the Algarve and the port of Faro. I go from village to village, engage in conversations with strangers, and set camp in new places every day. I am gifted a never-ending adventure on an ever-changing route, with new landscapes, a new sunrise, and the unknown at every bend. From the word go, this world run is everything I wanted it to be. I feel content, purposeful, driven, and extraordinarily happy.

On the seventeenth day of the run, I reach Seville in the early morning and continue my route towards Utrera, to the south of the city. It's a beautiful springlike day; I'm in my T-shirt, and the temperatures are mild. After my daily regimen of forty-two kilometers, I meet my family at a local tavern, and I'm euphoric. I didn't stand up to everyone or make a fool of myself. I'm happy to see them again. I jokingly say, "At this rate, we'll end up seeing each other more during this adventure than during my last two decades as a nomad!" This trip is already bringing us closer.

We reach the hacienda located on the heights of Seville, an old rustic building which will soon come alive with the hubbub of conversation and the excitement of my six nieces and nephews. I'm trying to rest a little. Before Christmas Eve, I have two marathons ahead of me, which will take me more than a hundred kilometers from the city. The WRA is definitive on this point. Every day, I must resume my run from the precise place where I left off the day before. Tomorrow, it will be the tavern, followed by Lebrija and Cuartillos, about thirty kilometers from Cádiz. I have jokingly appointed my father as Head of Logistics, and it will be his task to drop me off and pick me up every day. In truth, that's a lot of driving and a big responsibility.

On December 24, the whole family awaits me at the end of my run at noon. I have the children by my side for the last few hundred meters. What a joy! The setting is magnificent. We are in the middle of the Pueblos Blancos, the superb white villages that dot Andalusia's countryside. We sit down for a hearty meal of tapas and Spanish specialties, then head towards Cádiz for a sightseeing afternoon in the sun-drenched streets. Fourteen of us pose for a photo on the seafront for our first Christmas together in a long time.

I think about how this world run, having barely begun, has already fulfilled more than I could have imagined. Without it, we wouldn't be here all together. Although we are a united family, we each live our lives independently, and these occasions are rare. My siblings and I come from the same upbringing and the same home, yet we have taken vastly different paths. We have one thing in common, though. All four of us have followed our passions with determination and devotion. I feel that my world run stems from that same characteristic that binds us.

This is undoubtedly a hereditary trait, and my father certainly gave us the example of a career that he evolved according to his desires, opinions, and convictions. The unshakable stability of my mother, who worked in her pharmacy her whole career, undoubtedly constituted the pillar on which he could lean and give free rein to his convictions.

They met through the scouts in the 1960s, at a time when this movement was still a sign of the spirit of adventure and freedom. At the age of twenty, my father had already crossed former Yugoslavia by car, descended rivers on makeshift rafts, and pitched his tent in a multitude of countries, in all kinds of weather. Later, I saw him resign for a disagreement over principles, start a business, reinvent himself as the head of a management firm in a niche market, and establish his technical knowledge by serving as an associate professor at the university. In a way, he instilled in me this ability to do what I would later call my "leaps of faith."

We form an eclectic family where I don't stand out more than any other. My nomadism simply makes me a little more eccentric than the others. Eccentric in the literal sense. One that moves away from a given point, from a norm based on the founding of a family, and a stable geographical situation. I'm divorced, childless, and fidgety. For them, I am the free-spirited sister, the adventurous aunt, the one who allows herself adventures that they would not, or could not, have allowed themselves.

We spend one last moment together on December 25, a rest day for me, like every seven or eight days. Seville offers us the spectacle of the Plaza de España, its cathedral, and its Christmas lights, culminating in the lighting event on Constitution Avenue. These are precious moments, and I feel all the support and trust my family has placed in me. On the horizon, I am sure, many other reunions await. At least, that's what I believe. And perhaps a few surprises along the way.

5

FREEDOM IN EUROPE

Relieved to have honored this first appointment, it is alone, and with an appetite as strong as ever, that I continue my route towards the Iberian coast. I run through the isolation and dramatic settings of Zahara de la Sierra and Ronda, perched on breathtaking gorges and surrounded by pristine lakes. When I reach the Spanish coast, I suddenly join the more populated and lively resorts, which, in the off-season, still enjoy a fair amount of tourism.

My days end up structured around the same routine. I wake up before dawn and eat breakfast in bed in front of my computer. On the screen, I scroll through the day's stage. I memorize the route and its geographical particularities. I research the region and read a bit of its history, as well as the local news. An hour later, I'm up, loading my gear into the stroller. I put on the uniform that will follow me throughout the adventure: black shorts, a pink T-shirt, and a pink cap.

It may seem trivial, but I attach importance to having work clothes. I remember the time when my father set up his office in a room of the house. He got up every morning at dawn and always set about his working day impeccably shod and dressed in his suit and tie. My uniform is based on the same principle—it gives a form of structure to the day ahead. Maybe, sometimes, the clothes maketh the man, and with my pink cap screwed onto my head, there is no mistake. I am Lootie, the round-the-world marathon runner.

Why Lootie? I have spent my whole adult life in foreign countries where my surname has never been pronounced correctly. The nickname has stuck with me since my early days in Scotland, a mispronunciation of my surname, which is the closest locals would get to saying it right. For some reason, the same nickname followed me through all my expatriations. Other nicknames stuck for a shorter while, but Lootie is the one that has been used the most consistently. When choosing an address for my website, I decided to go with Lootie. There may be a million Maries around the world, but as far as I know, only one Lootie!

I hit the road, and the sensory experience begins. While waiting for my GPS to lock onto a satellite, I observe the morning dew, the quality of the daylight, the frost on the leaves of the trees, and the composition of the clouds in the sky. I feel the temperature on my bare skin and catch the scents of the air. Then, the effort accelerates my breathing and increases the coolness of the air that I swallow rhythmically. I adjust my stride on the back roads, trails, and dirt roads I take. As much as possible, I run in nature. During the first month, along the Portuguese and Spanish coasts, I navigate between the orange orchards and the seaside. I feel the pine needles that carpet the coastline under my feet. I listen to the songs of the birds. I watch for the animals that I surprise, and which hide or flee as I run past them. Every morning, the sun rises, facing me from the east. Every day, a new show, the splendor of which is for my eyes only to grasp.

This is how all the stages of this world run begin, and curiously, I no longer need an alarm clock. Far from being crushed by the fatigue of the runs, I wake up instinctively and excitedly every morning, anticipating the day ahead, the elements that I will be confronted with, and which will paint this new stage of the journey with a unique color. I often describe this world run as a fresco for the five senses. A subtle variation, day after day, of what I see, smell, taste, hear, and what I tread beneath my feet. Every day, a tablet encapsulates the sensations felt as I progressed and then joins the previous ones to preserve a unique experience of the planet in my mind.

Running like this in the open air gives a particular acuity to my relationship with the world, and if I can grasp all its beauty, it does not spare me its ugliness. It is naked before me, without a filter. In the second month of the journey, I reach the Almeria region in the South of Spain. I notice a change in the environment. I am no longer awakened at dawn by the song of birds. Nature seems withdrawn, dull, almost dead. I see scraps of plastic cartwheeling along the roads, accumulating on the coast, washed back by the sea like embarrassing ghosts. Before crossing El Ejido and its surroundings, I studied Google Maps, wondering what all that white area on the map could mean. I zoomed in on the screen without understanding. As I ran through it, I realized that these were dozens and dozens of kilometers of uninterrupted plastic fields.

I came across an incessant stream of immigrant workers criss-crossing the greenhouses in rags on their rusty bicycles. The El Ejido region is the pantry of Europe, the largest reserve of greenhouse fruits and vegetables on the planet. There, summer vegetables are produced in winter and tropical fruit all year round. This is how the world goes, and further beyond these fields of plastic, it's as if everything is forgotten.

Later, my route takes me straight to the Cabo de Gata Natural Park, a treasure trove of wild nature with spectacular coastal landscapes where flora and fauna thrive in complete tranquility. An earthly paradise at the gates of its evil twin, the hell of greenhouses and human stupidity. Sitting on the beach of Isleta del Moro that evening, deserted at the beginning of January, I grasped both its grandeur and its fragility.

As I run up the coast towards Valencia, I come across my first meteorological disaster. Storm Gloria is on its way to wreak havoc in the Mediterranean. I finish the run, barely able to push my stroller against the blizzard-like conditions. Exhausted, I take refuge in a local hotel restaurant, where I end up stranded for two days. I witness landslides, floodings, hail and snow, a trail of destruction that leaves over a dozen dead. When I resume my running, I see the damage firsthand. The most surprising sight may well be my run through the seaside town of El Grao de Gandia, where the back roads are peppered with dead fish. At first, I think maybe a truck carrying fish had overturned. That is before realizing that the sea had flooded the back roads and left all these fish stranded there. A devastating sight.

I follow the coast towards the Pyrenees for hundreds of kilometers, dressed in my uniform and stroller at arm's length. Past the beautiful city of Barcelona, I get to cross the Cadiretes Massif along its steep and rugged slopes, on the side of its low granite mountains, through its dense pine forests. I run alone through dozens of switchbacks, on a dizzying and stunning coastline roller coaster, my serenity only to be disturbed by the passage of the pelotons of professional cyclists who make this their winter training ground. They release clouds of dust as they pass and scare away the birds that sometimes accompany me on my way.

My parents drive across France to meet with me on the Spanish side of the border. The Pyrenees is my first big mountain crossing, and they have volunteered to help by transporting my stroller, while I run with only a small backpack on my shoulders. We spend three days together, and I realize how fortunate I am that they are so keen to support me and join me on my journey. As it turned out, I crossed the Pyrenees via the Col de Banyuls, on trails and at an altitude that would have been easy to run with the stroller. I did not need the help after all, but it was still very encouraging to see them and, once again, feel grateful for their company.

On the other side of the mountains, another country awaits, France. A new coastline presents itself to me, dotted with tourist sites that I am glad to cross out of season: Sete, Marseille, Cannes, Nice, etcetera. I am rediscovering a part of my own country whose lifestyle and culinary traditions I had missed so much. Running through the villages in the morning, I smell the aroma of freshly baked bread and croissants. Appreciating the slow pace of some of the remote places, where it seems old people sit in the main square, at the local café, all day long. I enjoy hearing French spoken in the streets. I have been away from my country for so long that it still takes me by surprise. I follow the numerous cycling paths that run along the coast, into the provincial areas and enjoy some quiet and peaceful running days.

With the Alps now looming in the distance, I notice that I have moved significantly away from my starting point, and I'm preparing to travel to a fourth country, Italy. When I enter on March 1, 2020, I already have 3,000 kilometers on the clock, and everything is going perfectly. While I'm happy about it, I also like to remind myself that I didn't leave my job as finance director to be dictated to by a preplanned Excel spreadsheet for two years. Give me something unexpected to spice this trip up! You should always be careful what you wish for.

I cross the border to Italy, past the town of Menton, and I am struck by the sudden change in my surroundings. The architecture, the colorful façades of the houses, the fresh air of the Alps cooling down the coastline. But this is not the only change that I notice. Throughout the beginning of my Italian wanderings, I read worrying news every morning. A virus from China is spreading through the country. Deaths. Confined cities. As I progress through the province of Savona on the Ligurian coast, the situation becomes complicated.

An outbreak of the COVID-19 infection has been detected. The hospitals are in panic. Hotels are closing. Hosts keep their distance. People cross the streets, hands over their mouths to avoid meeting others. I run through the heart of the problem, to the gates of the nest of contagions in Europe, and yet, surprisingly, I feel safe. Alone, and most of the time outside, I breathe in deeply the marine seaside air, pure and untainted.

Further east on the Italian coast, I face another storm with gusts of almost 100 kilometers per hour. It forces me to a halt for five hours. Dripping, shivering from the cold, I stop by the village of Andora and take refuge in the local hotel while waiting for the storm to pass. The managers' hospitality is remarkable. They offer me the use of their staff shower and served me a hot drink. Then, seeing lunchtime approaching, they bring me the dish of the day. I eat absentmindedly while observing the wind still howling outside, the palm trees almost horizontal. When I start to dive nose-first onto the table, they suggest I lie down in one of the vacant rooms. A few hours later, rested and warmed up, I notice that the storm is weakening. I get ready to leave, gather my belongings and realize that they had been left to dry during my nap. I thank the owner and take out my card to pay the bill. The man refuses with a hand gesture. I don't have to pay anything. He adds, "We have to close our doors this evening. It gives us great pleasure to know that our last gesture of hospitality was useful to you on your journey."

That afternoon, it is late when I arrive in Loano, my stopover point, and I am greeted by a closed hotel door. I look for an alternative on Booking.com. Nothing. It is all the more worrying when asking people for help is now, almost impossible. Everyone walks quickly, heads down and avoiding contact. I call the hotel number again and again. I'm outside, in my sweaty clothes, starting to feel fatigued. Someone finally picks up. In a mixture of English and Italian, the manager explains to me that the province of Savona is now in lockdown. Hotels are closing one after the other. There have been deaths in the region. I explain my despair. I am out on the streets, and this is my last night in the province. Tomorrow, I will be in Genoa. I don't know if he understands anything I say to him, but half an hour later he parks his car in front of the building.

I salute his courage. Fear seems to have settled everywhere, but he comes to meet me, to my rescue. Although he doesn't owe me anything (we have no masks, no protective measures), he loads my stroller and my bag into his trunk, then takes me to a guesthouse where I take the only room available.

"Tomorrow, everything closes here," he repeats. I spend the evening analyzing the news by translating the local papers. The situation is evolving day by day, and the measures taken are not yet unified, neither at the national level nor the regional or provincial level.

I keep going anyway. I have nothing else to do. Stop for what reason? Except for a few cities and provinces, I can still move around Italy and the rest of Europe in complete freedom. There is nothing to indicate, at this time, that the continuity of my journey is in any immediate danger.

As the days pass, the atmosphere becomes more disturbing and worrying. My arrival in Genoa is particularly striking. The streets are almost empty. The atmosphere exudes distrust; people take detours to avoid passing each other on the sidewalks. In the middle of a pedestrian street, a tramp is sprawled on the ground, looking around. He seems lost, and I wonder if anyone has taken the trouble to explain the situation to him. Genoa is the first of the "frozen cities" that I pass through. Life has deserted the streets, and the usually vibrant Italian urban landscape now looks abandoned.

My journey turns into a hurdle race and a constant challenge. Initially, fourteen Italian provinces are placed in lockdown for one month. During my daily marathons, I think about my schedule and my route. I turn them over in my head, still hoping to find a way to reach the opposite Italian coast, the Adriatic, and to cross into

Slovenia as quickly as possible. It is not yet clear whether other European countries are planning to resort to such drastic measures.

The inevitable happens. In Pisa, March 10, 2020, at the end of a magnificent stage of almost fifty kilometers under a warm spring sun, I check in at a local hotel. The receptionist hands me my key and a paper, a pass which will allow me to go to the train station the following day and then to the airport. I have been ordered to leave the country, which is now entering a complete lockdown. All travel is prohibited. A world first.

If I had been looking for a reason to end this world run, if these three months of running had been too hard for my liking, the pandemic could have served as an implacable excuse. An opportunity to capitulate easily. Quite the opposite is happening. The health crisis confirms my unwavering determination: whatever happens, I will see my adventure through to the end.

The thought of giving up never crosses my mind. I look for solutions and measure the potential impact of this pandemic on the rest of my journey, on my crossings of the continents and the concordance of the seasons. I understand that everything I had carefully calculated is now shattered. So what? I will adapt. I must go on. The unexpected, finally!

6

PANDEMIC

My steps echo on the Parisian cobblestones, punctuated by the ruckus of my stroller, which jerks from side to side, almost empty. Empty, like the streets I am running along. It is spring of 2020, and I spend my days running around the deserted capital, which looks like a cardboard film set. The world is at a standstill, time seems suspended, and lives are constrained between four walls.

From Pisa, I took a plane to Paris, an emergency repatriation, in a way. I moved into my parents' empty flat, and the first few days I was boiling with impatience, the inertia costing me greatly. Logically, I needed action and had to find a way to escape. The austerity of the measures in place only allowed citizens a daily exit authorization limited to one hour within a radius of one kilometer around one's home. All I could think about was how to resume my journey and, failing that, how to keep in running shape. Like everyone else,

I was in the dark. I had no idea how many weeks or months this imposed shutdown would last.

It is not just maintaining my physical fitness that worries me. After a few days of confinement, my mind short-circuits. I can no longer follow the flow of my thoughts or project myself into anything. Every action comes up against a wall of questions and unknowns, encouraged by the stream of continuous news that I watch from morning to evening. I need to find something to do quickly. Stranded in Paris, I realize how vital this adventure has become to me. Without this daily run, which pushes me forward each day, I feel stripped of my reason for being.

During this period of lockdown, most people are deprived of their freedom of movement, but they still have a house, a few belongings, a job for those who had one, and a routine. They retain some of their bearings. What is left for me, more nomadic than ever, without permission to move? Nothing. I am distraught. I'm not at home—I have never lived in Paris. I no longer have a house or any possessions. I do not have a job. The only thing I have is this freedom, this perpetual movement, and adventures from one city to another. It's all I have in the world. The confinement touches the heart of my being and stifles my soul.

I decide not to let this ordeal get me down, not to let these stern health measures destroy me. I will have to make myself useful and play a role during this pandemic that will live up to my identity as a globe-runner. After all, I have time on my hands; I have health and energy to spare. In these desperate times, I must be able to put my training and fitness to good use. I decide to turn to the service of others, not only to help but also to give myself a purpose. I apply to several volunteering platforms, and my efforts are rewarded. I am given a volunteer position and am responsible for collecting meals prepared by individuals and delivering them to the homeless people on the streets of Paris. The #PourEux (For Them) association had been set up at the beginning of the confinement, when most volunteers serving large charitable associations, most of them seniors, had been ordered to stay at home. I obtain a paper which symbolizes my newfound freedom, a certificate which authorizes me to travel twenty-four-seven around the city. From day one, I take all the tasks available on the association's application. I divide them into two rounds, one at lunchtime and the other in the evening. I deliver the meals by running, stroller in hand, like on the roads of the world. I cover between thirty and forty kilometers per day in this urban landscape tainted with a surreal atmosphere. I have never seen Paris from this angle, inhabited by a solemn, frozen beauty. The homeless people I meet are the only trace of life on the desolate streets. During my delivery rounds, I take ample detours to pass through all the districts of this capital that I know so little about.

This fabulous trip offers me a new gift. Paradoxically, this period of confinement and those that followed are among the most powerful moments of freedom of my adventure. I run and make myself useful. What a privilege! I get to meet the people who prepare the meals and the homeless to whom I distribute them. I am in the open air. I engage with strangers all day in the deserted streets of the most beautiful city in the world, while the majority of the population learns to live confined, distanced, and masked.

The pandemic signals a time to turn inward, the exact opposite of what I sought through this adventure. When I resume my journey, I notice that the bonds with friends and family have become much stronger. My good friend Laurence, who lives in Singapore, experiences the most severe health restrictions, lasting the longest in the world. We met in this Asian Pacific country during my last expatriation. With her husband, Yves, and their three children, we shared all the highlights of my preparation. I often ran from work directly to their home, where I had a place at their table, and more than once fell asleep on their sofa. They were like family to me.

From June 2020, calls from Laurence, still confined, become more frequent. She often calls me during my runs through the streets of Paris. I would turn on the video and, while running, share the landscapes around me, my sensations, and travel anecdotes. I understand her need to see and taste a little of my expedition. I am her breath of fresh air. She is my reminder of the privilege I have. I take on an additional responsibility. In this period of health restrictions, I am not only traveling for myself but also for those who, like Laurence, are under house confinement.

Until the end of my adventure, the evocation of this world run will elicit the most complete astonishment. Not so much because of the enormity of the running, but because I did so through a pandemic and the restrictions that came with it. The question I get asked the most is, "Didn't you think about giving up?"

As if it were unthinkable that this virus and its consequences could have allowed a solitary woman to slip through its cracks and travel across continents with complete impunity.

7

A SCORCHING SUMMER

Three months after the shock of the global lockdown, I am allowed to resume my run from Pisa, Italy, where I had stopped in March. The border controls have been partially lifted. Though I have managed to maintain my form throughout the confinement, I wonder what it will feel like to return to the road. The first months of the adventure went so perfectly well, so harmonious. I had found my legs, my rhythm, and a set of routines that had kept me safely and healthily on the road every day. Could the lockdown have jinxed the whole balance that I had established so carefully?

My thirst for adventure sweeps away these questions in an instant. I can't wait to return to my life out in the open and to my daily experiences, rich in discoveries. I had missed all the different intensities brought about by the voyage. Emotionally, in the discovery of the beauty in the world, nature, and encounters. Intellectually, in learning constantly about new places, about geography, history, and geology. Physically, in getting hooked to the high provided by the daily effort of a marathon. Sensorially, in inscribing within me the experience and memory of the journey through all five senses. I am ready as ever.

I decide not to go around the Italian coast, as initially planned, but to head in a straight line towards Istanbul. In two months, if all goes well, I should reach the shores of the Bosphorus, the gate to Asia. My main concern at this point is to limit the damage in terms of timing. This three-month delay is starting to have a significant impact on the concordance of the climates in the regions I have to cross. Since there is no indication, as of now, that the health crisis will have further repercussions or last much longer, I have to make my best effort to minimize the impact of the delay. If I manage to reach Istanbul in August, I will have to cross part of the Australian desert in the summer and cross the Andes under the snow, an almost impossible feat for any runner.

I cross Italy from Pisa to Trieste and prepare to enter Slovenia. Crossing borders on foot has become incredibly complicated, and I no longer enjoy the freedom of Europe as a single territory. I must present an entry form, a clean COVID test result (less than forty-eight hours old), and a passenger location form detailing my addresses in the coming weeks. There is no longer the guarantee that I can move around the continent as I please. Some land borders within Europe have now been closed. Hotel reservations are no longer secure; they can be cancelled at no notice if hosts or guests have been found to have contracted the virus. The logistical puzzle continues!

I turn the schedule over and over in my head. But as the weeks go by and summer catches up with me on the Croatian shores, it becomes clear that the other continents will not reopen their doors anytime soon. I change my strategy and opt for a long journey through Europe while waiting for the rest of the world to welcome travelers again. I have no idea how long it will take. How could I imagine that would be a whole year of additional running on the Old Continent in the making?

I retrace and change my route as I go. I'm now intent on running south down the Dalmatian coast, all the way around the coast of mainland Greece, and then crossing into Northern Greece. This should take me until the end of August. I will reassess my situation then. For now, the key is to savor the sweetness of the approaching summer. On June 21, the singing of the cicadas marks the arrival of high temperatures, and I quickly find myself in the grip of a heatwave.

The day I arrive in Split, Croatia, I pay a hefty price for it. For a week now, the temperatures have been soaring above forty degrees Celsius. I start my marathons a good hour before sunrise. I run out of the direct sun, often on coastal trails, shaded by trees as much as possible, letting the fresh air from the sea cool me down. But on that particular day, as the sun just started to peek over the horizon, my heartbeat accelerated rapidly, and my sweating suddenly took on unprecedented proportions. I wavered. Sitting in the shadow of a wall near the entrance to a supermarket, I grabbed my bottle of water to take small sips. I watched the sweat trickle onto the sidewalk, through my shoes, forming a puddle, and I couldn't do anything about it. Seeing my distress, a man came out of the supermarket and handed me a bottle of cold water.

It took me a good hour to get back on my feet and on the road. Learning of my misfortune via my daily blog, Tom Denniss kindly contacts me. He shares with me the trouble he experienced when he found himself in the grip of scorching conditions as he crossed the Western US during a heatwave. The problem is that humans are not able to regulate themselves when the outside air exceeds their body temperature of thirty-seven degrees Celsius. Our bodies have a fantastic array of tools, but we do not have air conditioning on board! It is, therefore, necessary to use external stratagems to help bring down the temperature and avoid hyperthermia.

I follow Tom's advice, and every morning, I put a block of ice in my cooler bag. The block melts naturally throughout the morning but slowly enough to last until the end. Whenever I start showing signs of overheating, I take breaks and apply the ice pack to my head while I cool down. The trick works, and I will use it throughout the summer along the Dalmatian and Greek coasts. I also become a shade hunter, constantly looking for any tree or wall to provide me with a bit of shade. The difference in temperatures between being in the direct sun and the shade can be as much as ten degrees Celsius, and in my condition, it makes all the difference. My run is often broken into segments, between two trees, and two ice-cooling breaks. The heat is crushing that summer on the Mediterranean coast.

I run a lot earlier. It's pitch black when I start, and my sensations are heightened. I hear the sea on my right, the sound of the fishing boats and the birds. The heat intensifies the scent of pine. My stroller is heavier, loaded with a few extra kilos of water. As the sun rises and the air ignites, the song of the cicadas heightens the sensorial experience of this first summer on the road. What a delight. In this first post-COVID summer, tourism has dived into free fall, and I am alone to appreciate the stunning beauty of this coast, along which a string of islands stretches as far as the eye can see: Brač, Hvar, and Orebić …

Once the daily run is over, a sweet reward awaits. I take my shoes and socks off, remove my sweat-drenched T-shirt, and dive into the coolness of the Mediterranean. I let myself float, surrounded by idyllic landscapes, and my body relaxes, quickly forgetting the rigors of the morning effort in the extreme heat. My tanned skin is exposed to the ferocity of the sun. The cap protects my face, but the rest of my body has changed color. Sunscreen is useless, as it washes away with all the sweating. After my swim, I sit on the terrace of a tavern, read the news, or prepare my daily report, and sip on a cold beer while waiting for lunchtime.

Very anecdotally, summer simplifies the question of laundry. In wintertime, I used to spend a good hour every day washing and then drying my clothes on hotel room radiators. It's quite unpleasant to start the day in damp clothes when the air is still cold outside. With the arrival of summer, my sweat-soaked clothes now go with me in the shower and then dry quickly at my bedroom windows. Being on the road does not mean being exempt from all domestic chores.

One more surprise awaits me in Dubrovnik, the Pearl of the Adriatic. My older brother and his young family have gone the extra mile to meet me here for a couple of days and then accompany me to Montenegro. I enjoy a little bit of family time, and I appreciate their efforts since traveling as a family has become incredibly difficult. On my rest day, we visit the ancient Venetian walled city together, almost devoid of tourists. The next day, as I cross into Montenegro, all three children run with me for the last few kilometers to my hotel. It will turn out to be the last time my family meets me on the road for a long time. But I do not know that yet.

Further south, the Albanian border brings about radical changes. As soon as I pass the border post, I find myself instantly deprived of an internet connection. Albania, I discover, is excluded from my European phone and data contract. I have to navigate by sight to find my hotel for the day. But it is not just the absence of data that takes me by surprise. I notice that everything around me is changing, and the country seems to live on another time scale. In the rural areas I pass through, I see people traveling in carriages pulled by horses or donkeys, on worn-out bicycles, and sometimes in rusty cars from another era. Around me, the minarets of the mosques have replaced the bell towers of the churches, Islam being the main religion here. A first on my journey and an exotic destination.

After the first night, I am awakened at dawn by the singing of the muezzin. A pleasant routine establishes itself to the rhythm of this musical call, allowing me to escape the oppressive temperatures. I trace my route through the countryside, the villages, and surrounding fields with the stunning Albanian Alps in the background.

I stand out in this landscape. Here, a jogger is not an ordinary sight. It is the sort of place where, if you are fit enough, you are expected to work in the fields. An old lady driving what looks like a timeless Škoda (an old Czech car model), parks in front of me. She gets out of the car and waits for me. With a broad smile lighting up her face, she hands me some pears. She must have just returned from picking because her car is filled with crates overflowing with fruit. She speaks to me in a language I don't understand and squeezes my hand in hers affectionately. I thank her in English. Then she rummages through the mess in her car and brings out a bottle of water. She hands it to me with tears in her eyes. I squeeze her hand to return her warmth. What could have moved this woman so much when she saw me? As I continue my run, I think about what her life must be like here, in the middle of the Albanian countryside.

Albania is the only country in occupied Europe that did not betray a single Jew during the Second World War. Better still, the Jewish population grew during that period. As I was to learn, this is all down to the Besa, the Albanian code of honor. I wonder if it is because of this code and her generation's natural protection of others that she recognized me as a foreigner and was so intent on showing me her warmth and hospitality.

On my second day in the country, I am lost on dirt roads amid a maze of fields and villages. Without access to the data on my phone, I only have static maps downloaded in advance. I'm a little confused. Google Maps has become my trusted guide, so much so that I am not used to navigating traditional maps anymore, and struggle to orient myself. A young boy wearing a straw hat, accompanied by his grandmother, comes out of the field on the edge of where I am sitting, followed by their flock of geese. I smile and wave at them to take a photo. They smile back at me. Seeing me lost, they offer to help. I show them the day's arrival point on the map, and they try to explain the direction to follow. But the language barrier gets in the way. They accompany me to the nearest village, followed by their poultry in single file. What a sight to behold! They take me across a small bridge made of two precarious wooden planks, too narrow for my stroller. The grandmother directs the operations while the boy grabs the thirty-kilo carriage, carries it above his head, and with the agility of a tightrope walker, crosses to the other side. They show me the way, then wave their hats as I leave, trailed by the cackle of their geese.

I appreciate the simplicity, warmth, and welcoming ways of this country. I also feel the poverty, precariousness, and wild natural beauty I did not suspect. I do not pass through the capital, Tirana, and choose to circumvent it instead. I see here and there what look like shanty towns, and on several occasions, stumble upon groups of people scavenging through garbage. A sad sight, casting a new light on this country, of which I had only seen the untouched beauty of nature and simplicity of rural life so far.

I join the coastline again in Vlorë. On this magnificent coast I follow, I feel myself sliding gently towards Greece. The markers appear subtly, in the food first, then in the language. I recognize more Greek words and finally manage to make myself understood here and there. This region of Albania has been the site of numerous battles between the two neighbors and bears many traces of Greek culture. The landscapes also change imperceptibly, and upon arriving in Sarandë, near the border, I notice that the coves and beaches look exactly like those of their Greek neighbor.

I await this crossing of Greece with great impatience. Once again, the border crossing in these times of COVID proves to be difficult. The land border is closed. So, I must run as close as possible to the border, abiding by the WRA rule, which states that a continent must be crossed "in a continuous line." Eventually, I take a bus back to Tirana, fly into Greece, and travel by bus again all the way back to the same border crossing on the Greek side. An extra cost and an unnecessary carbon footprint. But in this first summer of the pandemic, governments are trying all they can to limit mass tourist movements.

In the middle of August, I begin the tour of the Peloponnese from Igoumenitsa, in the very Northwest of Greece, which will see me follow the coastline all the way to Athens. The heat is overwhelming. My morning runs seem to drain my body of all its water, and I feel like a dry raisin at the end of each stage despite the six liters of water I consume. My swims in the Aegean Sea are such a beautiful reward, as well as a necessity to cool the engine down. The mark of my suntan, which stops abruptly at the height of socks, shorts, and T-shirt sleeves, is the only detail which distinguishes me from the surrounding vacationers.

I savor this crossing and revisit the past. When I was twelve years old, we toured the Peloponnese as a family. Three weeks of road trip and camping. My older brother sent me a copy of the map where he had noted all the stages, as well as the logbook that we had kept, where we took turns writing the day's report. During August, I retrace our journey thirty years later. I am amused by everything that surprised us at the time, by what seemed exotic to our young eyes. The hypnotizing, pure turquoise blue of the water, the mattresses of eucalyptus leaves on which we spread our sleeping bags at night to escape from the heat of the tent, the prickly pear cacti, the watermelon fields, the figs that we could pick directly from the tree, the arid landscapes, and the taverns where we enjoyed mezzes of local dishes in the evening.

As I get closer to Athens, I also reconnect with a more recent past. I'm going to meet my friends from the many years I lived here. I enter the capital at the Panathenaic Stadium, where, seventeen years earlier, I completed my first marathon. I glance at the shiny, marble stadium as I stop my GPS device and smile at it, "Hello, old friend. This time, it took me a lot more running to see you again!"

In the evening, we all meet at my good friend Lisa's house to celebrate our reunion with a festive dinner. Ah, and loads of the Greek wine I like so much. What a joy to finally take the world run on familiar territory; it is a first on my journey.

It is with a slight hangover that I hit the road again the next day, to retrace in reverse the route of the Athens Marathon. Starting from the capital's magnificent marble stadium, I reach the small seaside village of Marathon, forty-two kilometers to the east. Friends join my ranks and meet me at dawn near the stadium to accompany me all the way.

I finish my run at Dimitri's seaside resort, Moraitis Beach, in Marathon, then spend the afternoon relaxing and taking it all in. It is on this very beach that my life took such a dramatic turn for the better when I was twenty-six years old. That evening, Dimitris, his wife Vicky, and their children, Danae and Alex, invite me for dinner at the local taverna. We reminisce over the adventures we have shared over the years.

In 2007, I came back from Scotland for a weekend at the resort, ecstatic about completing my first triathlon at Loch Lomond. I must have spent the whole day just talking about how great it was and the joy I found in discovering this multisport. By the end of the afternoon, fired by my enthusiasm, Dimitris agreed to co-organize with me the first amateur triathlon in the country. He did not hesitate one second to provide me with all his support, help and encouragement.

We went through five difficult years together, and dozens of events, fighting against the authorities to give thousands of amateurs access to the joy of multisport, creating a community of like-minded people. It was an emotional roller coaster! It took a lot of work, but our joint efforts allowed the legitimacy of private organizers to be officially recognized in the country.

Over a scrumptious dinner of mezzes, washed down by a few bottles of local beer, we recount our adventures. I am grateful for Dimitris to have continued the legacy of the event after I left the country. That night, I stay in their beautiful house overlooking the Bay of Marathon for a well-deserved rest. At dawn, Dimitris drives me back to the beach, where I set out on my 157th marathon. The same place where, seventeen years earlier, I couldn't follow him on a five-kilometer loop.

8

TRACING MY ROUTE BETWEEN LOCKDOWNS

From Athens all the way up north to Thessaloniki, I seldom run alone. Word of mouth circulates amongst the running clubs about my venue, and little groups here and there join in to share a bit of the journey with me. I often find a few runners waiting for me at dawn in front of my hotel. I enjoy the company and meet a gallery of interesting and colorful characters. Quite a few women join me, including two who have run the renowned Spartathlon, the annual endurance race that connects Athens to Sparta in the spirit of the journey undertaken by the Greek runner Philippides. I am also joined for a day by Greece's ultra-endurance "Pope Runner," a bearded middle-aged priest who runs by my side dressed in his traditional Orthodox, heavy black robe.

At the end of my first summer of the world run, I finally hit Northern Greece. The land border with Turkey is still closed, so I decide to continue heading north and cross into Bulgaria via the Rhodope mountain range. I plan to run through the Balkans via

Serbia, Croatia, and Slovenia, then reassess my options given the pandemic situation. The world run is stalling in Europe, but it fulfils its function, and I do see the world beneath my feet.

On the other side of the mountains, I find myself again projected into another universe, the Bulgarian countryside. No more souvlakis, fresh fish and Greek salads, afternoons by the sea, or friends running alongside me. Summer ends abruptly. I now run alone among the mountains, vineyards, and on the dirt roads which connect a string of rural villages.

The experience of running through Bulgaria is quite peculiar. Though its capital, Sofia, is the image of a vibrant, modern, and cosmopolitan city, arriving on foot from the south and crossing the country at a slow pace gives me a vastly different perception of the reality of life there. I discover a relatively poor country. It is the second one in Europe, after Albania, where I notice people moving around on carts pulled by horses and donkeys. As I had noticed on approach to Tirana, the southern outskirts of the capital city seem to be where a lot of poverty is concentrated. I see what appear to be shanty towns and sewage running in pungent streams by the roadsides, in front of people's houses.

I then run out of the capital city, through the leafy and wealthy northern suburbs, and end up in beautiful, pristine countryside. What a stark contrast. All along the way, I am again the recipient of the wonderful hospitality of its inhabitants, their encouragement, and generosity. On the day before leaving the country to enter Serbia, I need to travel back to the capital city, Sofia, to get my COVID test results signed and stamped, one of the country's peculiar requirements. Before leaving, my host cooks me a meal to go, then accompanies me to the bus station and prepares a tray full of delicacies for my return. He knew that it will be late and that everything will be closed by the time the bus drops me off.

I catch up with the Danube River in Serbia, the natural border of the Balkans, and cross it again to enter Croatia. A few days before reaching Zagreb, I run all morning with a large building in sight. As I get closer, I identify a water tower. It plays hide-in-seek with me. The kilometers pass, and I realize that it is riddled with bullet holes, almost dilapidated, but standing. Imposing. Without its glaring scars, it would surely be nothing more than a disgrace to the landscape. But as it stands, it is stoic and commands respect.

Like Serbia, which I traversed earlier, I am touched by the well-ordained beauty of the landscapes, the green countryside scattered with big farmhouses. Animals roam free near cultivated fields. I enjoy my break times in this quiet environment. Sitting down by the side of the road, never far from a farm, I am invariably visited by the curious resident cat or dog. A few pats later, I am often met by the equally curious owner and, on occasion, invited in for a cup of tea.

How can I forget that twenty years ago, the entire region was shaken by the violent and devastating conflicts of the War of Independence, in such a beautiful and hospitable country? My thoughts wander as I pass the water tower to enter Vukovar, which under the crisp blue autumn sky, is resplendent. Appearances are deceiving.

The city is the very symbol of the war's atrocities. It was the subject of military relentlessness in 1991–1992, which brought it to its knees as the most bombed city in the conflict's history. Tanks are on display at the entrance to the city. I wander through the streets, which have also been preserved in addition to the dilapidated water tower and witness many traces of the fighting. I stop to touch bullet holes on the walls of partially reconstructed buildings with my fingertips.

I am struck by the vividness and freshness of my memories of the time. I see people my age and meet their eyes. They live in memory of the price they paid for their independence, a sort of living museum that is a reminder of their trauma. They lived their adolescence in the horror of the war, while I watched from the sofa at my parents' house, in the comfort and security of a country at peace. I am overwhelmed by Vukovar and its residents, who display their scars with pride, without misery, and who continue to live, without drama.

When I cross the Danube into Slovenia, the whole region is on the verge of another lockdown. I cross the border at the last minute, and two days later, the inevitable happens. Europe enters its second wave of lockdown, that of autumn–winter 2020. I continue my run to the city of Maribor, on the border with Austria, a stunning city set on the banks of the Drava River. Beautiful, but now forbidden, and in full lockdown. For the second time since the start of this world run, I am ordered to pack my gear and stop my running. I decide to take shelter in Greece, at my friend Lisa's.

Like the first lockdown, I prioritize finding an activity to keep myself busy, be useful and keep fit. I conveniently find a volunteer position at the Goodwill Caravan in Athens, an NGO which helps migrants with administrative and legal matters. I help with translation services, mostly. The job itself doesn't entail any running, but it comes with a twenty-four-seven circulation pass, and I can commute on foot to cover reasonable distances every day. I enjoy Lisa's hospitality, and being with a friend makes the lockdown experience a lot more bearable.

At the beginning of December, France surprises all its neighbors by ending what will be its last lockdown of the health crisis. I leave Greece by plane to resume my trip from Valence, a town I ran past in my crossing of France's Mediterranean coast, to begin a south-to-north crossing of France. I imagine that by the time I reach the north of the country, other countries will have opened their borders, and I will finally be able to take a beeline to Istanbul. At least, that's the plan!

Traveling extensively through France had never crossed my mind. I am not at odds with my country, even though I left it long ago. This improvised itinerary intrigues me and gives me a spring in my step. I pass through Lyon, the magnificent ancient city that I have never seen before, make my way along the River Rhone, through the wine-making region, then on to Sancerre, a gem of a tiny wine-producing city perched on a hill. My strides take me into Auvergne and the Loire Valley, through a network of cycling and riverside paths. I enjoy the variety and history-filled richness of the countryside and the medium-sized towns of my country, which I know so little about.

On December 31, 2020, the weather is frigid, and the fields are covered in frost as I leave Orleans at dawn on my way to Châteaudun, fifty kilometers away. As I approach the city, I check the contact details of my host for the day on my cell phone and realize that my accommodation has been cancelled without notice. Worryingly, I find no other options for lodging in the vicinity. It is freezing outside, and I don't have my camping gear onboard anyway.

I decide to send a message on Facebook, a shot in the dark. A little miracle happens, the vice-mayor picks up the call and takes it upon herself to organize my welcome at short notice. A little reception is arranged at the city hall, at the end of which, Marianne hands me the keys to the local lodge. I have tears in my eyes as I accept her gift. What's better than a roof, a meal to share, and the warmth of a festive welcome to end the year in style?

Further north, I meet with my brothers and parents in Paris. A little over a year earlier, we celebrated Christmas and the start of the world run together in Seville. They point out humorously that in one year, I haven't gotten very far! They are quite right, and though I am getting close to 10,000 kilometers of running, I am still technically very close to Portugal. On the day I arrive in Rouen, a reception awaits me despite the current regulations that forbid gatherings of more than eight people in France.

My sister contacted the mayor's office, who then organized a few local athletes and citizens to join me as I run into the mediaeval city. And who better than Serge Girard to welcome me? How uncanny that two of the seven world runners should originate from the same city of Rouen in Normandie, France!

He joins me with a contagious smile (partly hidden by his face mask). We chat as we make our way into town, surrounded by dozens of runners. A marvelous opportunity to catch up with friends and family again.

This month and a half across France has been a welcome catch-up lesson on the riches and diversity of my home country, as well as the hospitality of its inhabitants. By inviting itself on the journey, the unexpected has offered me a lovely surprise, reminding me there is no need to go far to travel and discover.

I pursue my route east towards Belgium. As I reach Namur, I celebrate the 10,000th kilometer of the world run. It is a strange and mixed emotion. I would never have expected to be stuck in Europe for so long and be so close to my starting point when celebrating that landmark. The local Burgmeister and a few journalists are gathered at the cathedral square to welcome me. The next morning, having read of my adventure in the local paper, two young guys in their twenties await me at the restart of the run. They plan to run about fifteen kilometers with me, which is very kind of them.

We get going along the local green corridor, and they tell me their story. They had been planning to run their first-ever marathon last year, but COVID happened, and all races were cancelled. The two friends felt disheartened that their training had all been for nothing. The occasion to run by my side is the first time they have found the motivation to get out and exercise in a long time. I ponder this as we plod along. Approaching the fifteenth kilometer, I gently challenge them to run a further six kilometers by my side, so they will have the satisfaction of having run a half-marathon. Our pace is slow, the weather is perfect, and we're having a good time. They keep going.

As we hit the half-marathon mark, I have another chat with them. The furthest they have ever run in training is twenty-seven kilometers. I challenge them to go a bit further and hit thirty clicks, a nice round number that will make this day even more special. They are in good shape, we are still having fun, and they agree.

As we reach kilometer thirty, I throw them the ultimate challenge, to run the last twelve kilometers by my side. It takes a little more convincing, but eventually they accept. What joy to see these two young lads, without much training, pulling a full marathon. It goes to show if the mind is in the right place, the body will follow. I often think of Jeremy and Valentin and the extraordinary resources they found within themselves that day.

By the middle of winter, I am faced with the impossibility of continuing further east. The tourism industry is still at a standstill in Germany and Austria. I head south and leave Belgium through the Ardennes Mountains in a terrible snowstorm and foggy conditions. I have no choice but to keep going south, and I see Switzerland as a great opportunity to catch up with more friends.

It's early spring when I cross into Geneva on a beautiful sunny day. The surrounding snow-capped summits are imposing and provide a superb background for the upcoming reunions. I catch up with a bunch of friends and ex-colleagues from my time working in Zurich, as well as friends I met in various expatriations. A four-week-long tour of friendships in short! It is no wonder why so many foreigners choose to live and work in Switzerland. The quality of life is rich, and the environment is breathtaking. Every day feels like I'm running in a postcard through the forests, skirting lakes and valleys.

9

VILLA VETTA

I hurtle down the side of these hospitable mountains, which are now so familiar to me. I've been exploring them for almost a month, along their paths, into the depths of their green valleys, through their massifs, and crossing their snow-capped peaks. I've finally arrived in Italy. I feel it. I didn't cross through a border post, but the atmosphere has changed. The architecture, the colors, the smell of coffee, the sounds of this lilting language bursting through open windows or the conversations of passersby. Everything around me is different.

Through the town of Verbania, I slow my pace to better absorb this new environment. The horizon is clearing, and the mountains now share the scenery. The waters, whose course I followed for kilometers, gather at their feet in an immense sheet that extends as far as the eye can see. I stop my run for a moment and sit on the shores of this blue expanse, Lake Maggiore.

The air is cool, but the morning sun burns my cheeks. I give myself a break and stare into the distance at what awaits me. For now, the grueling climbs are over. I will run on the paths along the lakes, on flat ground, reconnecting with my tempo, averaging a little over nine kilometers per hour. It's the pace I have adopted over the 295 marathons it has taken me to get here.

I resume my running, hands clinging to the handlebar of my stroller. It contains everything I need for this adventure. It also carries all I own. I have given up all my possessions for this trip. I have become free from all forms of attachment. Fully loaded, the stroller weighs around thirty kilos and has made me work tirelessly on the slopes of the Alps. Soon, my arms will be as muscular as my legs! This is no ordinary stroller. Practical and robust, it is equipped with shock absorbers and three bike wheels fitted with all-terrain tires. It's an American model called the "Beast of Burden" (Bob), which gives a good idea of what it can support. I nickname it Bob and think of it as my faithful traveling companion.

I look ahead to the lake, Il Lago Maggiore. The musical sound and rhythm of these words, the exaggerated, drawn-out ending, "Lago madjoooore," are familiar to me. They resonate in my head, bringing back a flood of memories. Somewhere on these banks is a villa, of which I have heard so much about. I have never seen it, but I know it is on the heights of Ascona, a town in Ticino, Italian Switzerland, where I will make a detour. My steps bring me closer. I accelerate, impatient to discover it. I can't help but think that this distant home played an essential role in my desire for elsewhere.

At the end of a cove, I see a row of brightly colored houses, red, blue, green, yellow, and pink, which stretch out like a candy necklace along the coast. The bell tower of a church overlooks them. In the background, the scenery of the Alps and their snow-capped peaks. It looks like a postcard. Timeless. The closer I get, the better I visualize the outlines of the city set at the foot of these imposing mountains.

I leave the banks of the lake and enter the heart of Ascona. My stroller jerks on the cobblestones; it vibrates with me, almost toppling over at each turn. I slalom between passersby and glance from side to side, looking for a sign, but I get lost in the streets. I climb up the paths that lead to the highest points but go around in circles. I ask for help.

A museum employee gives me the information I need. I follow her advice and run up the Monte Verità alley, lined with cherry blossoms. I pass by large mansions leading up to a spiral path protected by a wrought iron gate. It's open, so I rush in, making my way amongst the sparse vegetation dotted with immense palm trees. I reach the top and stop abruptly. It faces me, dazzling and majestic. I am touched to the heart.

Villa Vetta is aptly named ("vetta" means summit in Italian) and stands out vibrantly against the vivid blue sky. It is more opulent than I imagined, even more beautiful. I catch my breath while taking it all in. What a sight! I ring repeatedly, leaving my finger pressed for ten seconds on the doorbell button. No one home. No one to explain why this house is so important to me, or why I need to visit it. I will have to content myself with the outside.

The bright yellow façades contrast with the stern contours of the white-painted balconies and windows. The central building rises over three floors, adjoining two other units. The east wing, the largest, boasts several arcades, housing a covered veranda. The more austere west wing sets its back to the mountainside, adorned with closed shutters.

My Grandmother spent part of her youth here, six months a year. It was her father's house. I walk around it several times, and I can almost see the scene of that stormy evening. The house, high up and exposed while my grandmother, lying in bed as a child, tries to fall asleep. The windows open to escape the crushing humidity. When suddenly, a lightning bolt flashed into the room and crossed it from side to side. I imagine her fear, a trace of what always troubled her eyes when she told me that story.

I try to remember everything I know about this house. When I was younger, I often asked my grandmother to tell me about her villa in Ascona. I listened with emotion and imagined this lake and these mountains as an exotic universe conducive to a thousand adventures. Seeing it as an exceptional playground, rich in lessons and opportunities.

A touch of disappointment always seized me when my grandmother mostly talked about her boredom, the Italian lessons that she hated and her father, my great-grandfather, a whimsical and angry character who made her life difficult. She, who cultivated the art of conversation so well, was surprisingly short on the history of her childhood.

Yet, it is here that this formidable woman grew up between two cultures, and two countries. Yolande Righetti, my father's mother, chose Paris and the Sorbonne to continue her studies in chemistry, at a time when devoting oneself to sciences was not an obvious path for a woman. She then married a man promised to another, a fault blamed on her and not on him.

At the time my grandmother told me her Swiss Italian stories, she had just retired and left the direction of the Marguerite-Durand library—the first and only establishment in Europe dedicated to the history of women, feminism, and gender. In 1964, when she took over as director, piles of books, magazines, documents, and flyers populated the shelves. She made it her mission to bring this place of culture and history to life. Order, document, list and enrich. Share.

I have always known her with her nose buried in books, endless piles of which rose on either side of the armchair that she seldom left. Just like her glasses, held around her neck by a loose cord. She would sometimes suddenly stop reading to share her opinions with me. She had a wonderful ability to become instantly passionate about what she had just read.

One day on vacation, while I was reading alongside her, she placed her book on her knees with panache and called out to me, her finger outstretched, "Do you realize, at that time, a woman had to have the consent of her husband to use a bank account!"

But what era is she talking about, I wondered? She was talking about France before 1965. I understood that my grandmother, without having been a real activist or militant, was always one of those women who never accepted the place society reserved for them. Not only in her fields of predilection, sciences, and literature, but in all spheres of society. Very subtly, she awoke my conscience. I, too, will build projects that live up to my dreams and ambitions, and not to the supposed limitations of my condition as a woman.

As I leave Ascona for the rest of my journey, I let the memories of these afternoons of reading pass by. It is on my grandmother's bookshelves that I discovered all the titles and authors that evoked elsewhere and became so important to me. She never forced my choices, letting me choose as I wished: John Fante, Jack Kerouac,

John Dos Passos, William Faulkner, Ernest Hemingway, and John Steinbeck. It was all so far from the boredom of my high school reading lists that I immersed myself in these books.

I discovered a gallery of freedom-loving characters, tracing their paths. From the uprooted Bandini, away from his Abruzzo, to the celestial tramps of Kerouac. I wandered with them in a maze of adventures, so far from everything I knew. The unknown, the travels, the peculiar life choices outside of established patterns, it was all there.

My literary wanderings cost me a serious setback. I took the French literature baccalaureate, having read none of the books in the program. The scores I obtained were in line with this masterful impasse. Despite my father's crestfallen expression upon receiving my pitiful scores, I had no regrets. Where would I be today without those authors whom I took as guides, who served as mentors to me? Would I have allowed myself the choices that made me flee a well-ordered life? Would I have undertaken this world run?

At fifteen, I unearthed a book by Steinbeck, *Travels with Charley: In Search of America*, from my grandmother's shelves. The first phrase immediately caught my attention. The author whispered in my ear and, with humor, came to seal my fate. "When I was very young, and the urge to be someplace else was on me, I was assured by mature people that maturity would cure this itch. [...] Nothing has worked. [...] I fear the disease is incurable."

10

ITALIAN SHENANIGANS

Having rounded Switzerland, and with the borders to the East of Europe still firmly closed, I decide to head further south for a tour of the Italian coast. I figure that by the time I finish, it will be early summer, and the situation around the borders is bound to be different. I have already spent over a year crisscrossing my way around Europe. I am hoping things will change and that I will be able to continue my journey in the direction I must.

The West Coast of Italy provides me with quite a bit of an adventure. Rome certainly stands out as a highlight. I enjoy a rest day in the city of ruins, walking through this open-air museum all by myself: the Colosseum, the Trevi Fountain, and the Vatican, all with no tourists around. I feel the absolute privilege of getting to discover these places on my own, in silence. Of course, the downside is that all the cafés and restaurants are closed, and there is something amiss not being able to suck in the atmosphere and shared experience of the place.

The next day, I leave Rome via the old Appian Way, one of the most ancient Roman ways, preserved with its original large, shiny, slippery cobblestones. It is a tough, back-breaking exercise to run on it with the stroller. It's twice as hard on my arms and core work, but the reward is worth the effort and pain.

I cut through the countryside and enjoy the spectacle of ancient Roman ruins scattered by the side of the path alone, in the wilderness of untouched nature. An air of time traveling pervades. Had I crossed the country by car, train, or bike, I would never have experienced that Appian Way. I appreciate even more the value of traveling on foot, of spending time to enjoy and understand what links one place to another through geography and history, and how we are all connected. With these pleasant thoughts, I continue my route south towards Napoli. I certainly was not expecting what came next.

I notice the coastline begins to look abandoned, neglected. Seaside buildings, which must have been in their prime in the '70s or '80s, stand empty, washed-out, and paint peeling off their faces. The atmosphere is different, a stark contrast from the vibrancy encountered further north through Milan, Bologna, and Rome. A few days into the coastal run, I stop by the town of Castel Volturno. I will never forget this name. The whole run leading to it felt like I was in a no man's land. Substantial quantities of garbage littered the side of the road, waiting prostitutes scattered here and there, sitting on chairs, and looking bored. When I make it to town, everything around me (buildings, streets, fields) is derelict. A ghost town.

I must have found the only room for rent available in the region, located in a gated property. I feel fidgety, and I ensure the locks in my room work. After a quick nap, I make my way to the only store in town, a little corner shop selling groceries. Five imposing men stand guard and follow me through every alley I walk. Cash payments only. I walk back home with my packet of pasta and sauce. Around me, refugees carry old mattresses and broken furniture, meet to cook around an open fire, and scavenge from the piles of rubbish. It seems the city itself, and everything in it, has been abandoned by the country. I wonder how these people live here and what they must think of us and Europe. Certainly, a far cry from a promised land and a very sad sight.

Past Napoli and Pompeii, I make my way to the East Coast, cutting through the Apennines, which will be the backdrop of a real fight against the elements. Early one cold morning, I find myself running at the foot of the mountains under a heavy rain. I shiver, and my clothes become soaked. The skies are grey and low. In front of me, the Miscano River blocks my way. I don't see a bridge. I'm stuck, alone, in the middle of nature. With the tip of my frozen fingers, I consult Google Maps on my phone, the shoddy oracle that has gotten me this far.

I see no alternative to the path I have embarked on. The wisest solution would be to retrace my steps back to Benevento, from where I started this morning. Go back eighteen kilometers in the opposite direction just to take shelter and plan for another route. In short, a day of thirty-six kilometers for nothing. I hesitate and sit on the wet gravel beside the river, zooming in and out on my smartphone screen.

I curse the app which, with a clear blue line on the screen, assured me an easy passage, erecting an imaginary bridge over the Miscano River. I ponder for a while, then stuff my phone back in the bag. My decision is made, "Chi va piano, va sano e va lontano." (He who goes slowly, goes safely, and goes far). We will get there!

I decide to cross the freezing river. I take out my bag in its waterproof protection and fold my stroller. And in I go, up to my waist, with no idea of what lies at the bottom of the river. I simply hope not to slip and lose my equipment. Three trips are necessary to get everything across. This little adventure has galvanized me. I no longer feel the cold. This isn't the first time I've made the observation that when everything goes south, I feel most alive, and able to measure the extent of my resources. In this moment, the old me fades away into the far distance, the serious financial director in her pretty dress and heels, contemplating the bay of Singapore from her cozy office. The image makes me smile.

Having overcome these difficulties, I put my stroller back in order. The rain is still falling hard. A few hundred meters away, the path I'm running on stops abruptly and disappears. To my left, three meters of void separate me from the river below. To my right lies a soggy field on a very steep incline. Turning back is now even more out of the question. I put aside the rising concerns engulfing me and draw a line mentally on the side of the sloped terrain. To hell with Google Maps, I'm going for it! The decision goes awry, and my stroller escapes me. I contort myself to catch it, slip, and end up face down in the mud, saving the stroller from slipping down into the river, holding on to it for dear life.

Once I recover, I go through the next few hundred meters with mixed success, covered in mud and scratches. The cold grips me again, but I continue. Not only does the adventurer in me wake up, but the competitor reveals herself. It's me versus the elements today! Another path emerges further up the road, and I welcome it with excitement.

Take that on the chin, Google Maps! I'm going to make a joke of your perfect blue line itinerary to Savignano Irpino, my haven for the night! What exactly were you thinking? That I was going to turn away at the first difficulty? Did you take a good look at me? Have you seen this river? Have you seen this slope on which I danced with so much grace to reach the path that now offers itself to me? How good I feel right now!

People often ask me if I suffer from loneliness on the journey. If only they knew! In this epic adventure, everything is a conversation: with my environment, the fauna, the flora, the sky, the sun or the rain, everything that surrounds me. I even talk to my wacky oracle, that damn Google Maps. How can I be bored for a moment? Boredom may be found in offices, comfortable chairs, and careers. But here? Never.

I only have thirty kilometers of running left, and I am wrong to think that the hardest part is behind me. A few strides later, I am again at a standstill. The three wheels of my stroller are now trapped in a layer of heavy, sticky clay. I crouch down to assess the damage and go for it with both hands. I remove the clumps of mud stuck on the wheels but also under my soles. I feel nailed to the ground.

I get going again, but the clay slows me down after a few meters. I repeat the operation several times. I struggle over the next six kilometers for almost three hours under the heavy rain. An eternity. It's exhausting, yet it never occurs to me to give up. I think of my predecessors, the other six people who have already run around the world and all the challenges they had to face. Among them is Serge Girard, who made his motto this quote from French humanist Théodore Monod, "To live is to move forward, always." Today, Serge and Théodore whisper in my ear. I am moving, so I am alive. It's slow, but I'm making progress!

When I eventually get back to an asphalt road, I have never been so happy to see some bitumen. The road rises like a crescendo. With its reputation as the most beautiful village in Italy, Savignano Irpino, perched at an altitude of 727 meters, takes on the appearance of a holy grail. It's still raining, my clothes are sticking to my skin, and I am shivering. I'm also starting to get hungry. I left at half past seven this morning, and it's well past the lunch hour when I usually finish my daily marathon. On the final climb to my destination, I wonder if I will find a place to buy food this evening. I don't have any reserves on board. In these days of the pandemic, getting supplies is no longer a simple task.

I end up bent in half under the weight of my thirty-kilo stroller which, on the hill, seems to weigh over a hundred. I'm at the end of my strength. There are no hotels available in Savignano Irpino. I had booked a room through Airbnb and informed my host of my delay. I stop running in front of the only trace of life in the village, a stationary car, engine running with a fluffy cloud of smoke escaping its tailpipe. I see a man behind the wheel, "Are you Pasquale?"

"Si!" His face expresses all his astonishment. I'm soaked in sweat, covered in mud, and pushing a baby stroller, exhausted by the effort. What a spectacle I offer him!

He accompanies me to the room that I have rented for the night. Before he leaves, I take the liberty of asking him if he can get me some pasta and cheese, as the village store is closed, and I have nothing left to eat. Pasquale reassures me he will be back within thirty minutes with some supplies. I shut the door, get rid of my soggy clothes that are heavy with mud, and head for the long-awaited shower. The pleasure is brief. The water is lukewarm and turns downright cold within minutes. It doesn't matter. I'm clean and dry.

Pasquale returns with a packet of spaghetti, a piece of parmesan, and some biscuits. I thank him profusely, and he disappears. But as I put the water to boil in the kettle, a sharp click resonates. The fuse box has blown. I look for the electric panel but in vain.

"Hello, Pasquale?" Here he is again, ten minutes later. The panel is located outside, in a courtyard to which I do not have access. He then checks the room. I have plugged in my computer, cell phone, two GPS devices, and the batteries for my satellite beacon. The lights are on, and I am also using the small electric heater. It's too much. He explains to me that I will have to sleep without heating. It's -5°C outside. The night promises to be as harsh as the day.

When dinner is over, I lie down in the dark and cold and think back to John Fante's hero, Bandini. Far from his native Abruzzo, a beautiful region that he sometimes describes with nostalgia, and whose poverty he wrote about. I am only about a hundred kilometers south of this region. I imagine that the landscapes I have just run through today resemble those from which his character came, with his empty pockets and full heart. He, who followed his path with a beautiful mixture of naivety and insolence. He never stopped putting distance between himself and his roots, guided by his ideal of living his American dream as an accomplished artist.

I am on his land, and despite the difficult conditions of the day, I am thankful for this world run. It makes me cross the paths of my ancestors and the heroes of my readings. I've run through icy rivers, discovering these villages in which I would never have set foot in otherwise, and draw on resources that I did not suspect.

"Know thyself," I hear Socrates murmur. This trip never ceases to surprise me.

11

ISTANBUL, AT LAST!

At the end of May 2021, as I conclude my run around Italy, a wind of freedom blows around me again. Europe is getting out of lockdown for the second time, and summer is approaching. Good news finally reaches my ears as the land border between Greece and Turkey reopens. I run my last Italian steps in Trieste and quickly hop on to Thessaloniki, a city I passed through when I started my way up the Balkans the previous September. The WRA requires that any continent be run in a continuous line, from one side to the other, but it does not matter how many dead ends one hits. I set off on the last section of my European crossing.

I find myself in the grip of all kinds of emotions. For a year and a half, I have been traveling the countryside and the coastline of this wonderful continent. It has fulfilled me in return. Every morning at sunrise, tirelessly, I've soared with my senses wide open to the elements and listened to all the lessons the road had to offer.

I've discovered the richness of the continent's history, the diversity of its architecture, the splendors of its geography, the mystery of its borders and the secrets they conceal. I've tasted the figs and peaches picked from the sweet-scented trees of Greece in the middle of summer, and I've battled in the snow and fog across the Ardennes. I've met people, men and women who opened their hearts and their homes to me, with whom I shared bread and a little of their dreams. My friends and loved ones have showered me with their trust, their support, their love, and their friendship.

At the end of June 2021, ten months later than planned, with 15,500 kilometers on the clock and four cumulative months of layoff in confinement, I finally have the Bosphorus and its Golden Horn in sight. I feel like a weight has been lifted off my shoulders. For as long as I have been wandering in Europe, I have experienced a form of imposter syndrome regarding the journey. I did not allow myself to voice that I was traveling around the world. After all, was I not just trying to get to Istanbul while navigating the impossible maze created by the pandemic? When people asked me what I was doing, I often replied, "I'm running to Istanbul," as if it were still illegitimate, at this stage, to declare that I was on the path of a much more grandiose odyssey.

It is only by concluding the first continental crossing to tackle the second, that the adventure finally takes on its global dimension. I feel relieved and comforted. The idea of giving up has never crossed my mind. Desire, my fuel, has given me an unfailing drive and propelled me against all odds.

I had initially planned to celebrate my continental arrivals in a small group, with family or friends. But COVID has changed all my plans, and nobody can travel to meet me in Istanbul. The idea of a solo finish, with no one there to celebrate with, is a prospect that doesn't thrill me. So, with a shot in the dark, I send an email to the contact section on the website of the Consulate of France in Turkey. To my surprise, magic happens.

In the last ten kilometers of the run, I meet a French journalist and Gabriel, a representative from the consulate. He has arranged to gather a group of runners from the city's marathon club. We all meet at the small Saint Sophia Mosque, and our little group runs across the Galata Bridge, entering the heart of the city together. How resplendent!

Under a blazing sun, at the bend of some of the many small alleys that scatter the historical center of the city, we cross the gate of the Palais de France, where a guard of honor awaits me. The consul is here, with all his staff. I am elated and oh, so happy not to be alone for this major landmark.

The moment of exchange that follows, allows me to realize the enormity of what I am doing, in itself, and given the circumstances. It's time for a first assessment. My head rushes with all the fantastic moments I have experienced over the past year and a half. I try to transcribe the intensity and all-encompassing freedom of this trip into words, despite the emotion that grips me.

Following administrative complications due to the health crisis, I am required to spend a week in Istanbul before flying to Seattle and, thus, begin my journey across North America. The ambassador lets me settle in at the Palais de France, and I have a floor to myself in this magnificent building where the consul and his wife also have their quarters. In the empty corridors of this historical building, I set out to test the camping equipment I will need in the United States. Thank goodness I am alone. The sight of a tent pitched right on the polished parquet floor lounges could have raised a few eyebrows!

During this imposed break, I make a few useful visits. First, to the pupils of the French school of Istanbul. We spend the afternoon together, and they take me around their beautiful school, perched on a tree-covered hill with views out to the sea. I have been in contact with a few schools since the start of the journey, some in Singapore, Switzerland, and France.

I enjoy sharing with young children. I recognize the excitement they feel at the simple evocation of a "trip around the world." They also ask funny questions. A young girl keeps raising her hand, waiting for her teacher to allow her to talk. She is stammering with excitement when it is her turn, and she asks, "Did you have to go fishing in rivers to get some food on your journey?"

Sheepishly, I answer that, like herself, I have been buying my food in shops so far. I could tell she was disappointed, and that my journey was not as wild as her imagination had let her believe!

I also meet the activists from the NGO Kader, which works for gender equality. This is a significant mission, as Turkey withdrew from the Istanbul Convention (Council of Europe Convention on Preventing and Combating Violence Against Women and Domestic Violence) in 2021.

I listen to them tell me about their struggle. These women have a long path ahead of them. Gender equality in the workplace is no way near as advanced as in their European neighbors. I feel all the privilege I inherited, having been raised in an environment and culture where I did not have to fight for the relative equality from which I benefit.

It took the efforts, determination, and struggles of the women from my grandmother's and mother's generation to get to where I stand now. This meeting is an occasion to share about the phenomenal capabilities and resilience of women, and I fear their journey will be much longer than my world run. I am even more determined in my commitment to put my endeavor, loud and clear, to the service of this just cause.

I spend my last day in Istanbul in the company of Sayeh, the consul's wife. She is an accomplished artist of Iranian origin, as well as a trained architect. I discover her meticulous, intricate, and poetic creations, which she has exhibited in art galleries across Europe. Discreet, almost shy, and funny, Sayeh opens her drawing boxes to me, showing me her latest projects. I understand that art is her freedom. It is her outlook on the world, her expression as a strong woman beneath her self-effacing appearance.

Her parents, who are visiting, join us later in the afternoon. I receive two pairs of earrings, handmade by Sayeh's mother, who is an artist too. All three are fascinated by my world run, and I try to answer all their questions, transmit my motivations, and the desire for the open road that drives me, while I watch their reactions and shining eyes. The emotion is palpable.

Iran, where Sayeh is from, is another country where women do not enjoy the same rights as men under the terms of Sharia law. I probably represent an image of emancipation, of a woman free to travel as I please, living outside of norms and clichés. In their company, I feel the strength of what my journey means to them.

Once I completed my European leg, I should have reached Southeast Asia for a crossing of the Malay Peninsula, to the southern tip of Singapore. Then ran across Australia, in the logic of a west–east circumnavigation, before getting to North and South America and returning to my starting point via a crossing of the

North African coast. The plan would have allowed me to run on each of six populated continents, and cross four of them entirely, from ocean to ocean.

But the global health crisis continues to change my plans, and when I finally reach Istanbul, the entire Asia-Pacific region keeps its doors closed. I appeal to the WRA and am granted a special exemption. I will go to the only continent open to travelers at this time, North America.

The border between the United States and Canada is no longer crossable as I had imagined, and I have to review my itinerary once again. I decide to stay in Uncle Sam's country for the whole crossing, since I already have a ten-year visa. Obtaining a tourist visa for Canada at this time would be mission impossible.

I leave Europe with a pang in my heart and a touch of apprehension. I will now be isolated, on a continent where I don't know anyone. The distances from city to city are of a completely different magnitude. I will have to push the kilometer cursor, and there will be nights of camping in the wilderness and in the grandeur of the national parks.

I cannot wait to get to grips with it and discover the immensity of this continent that I know so little about. I land in Seattle, and the border officer asks about my profession. I don't skip a beat and answer, "Athlete."

He continues, "Business or leisure?"

"Leisure," without hesitation!

12

NORTH AMERICA, INTO THE UNKNOWN

I set off from Seattle, outward bound from the Puget Sound, with the Pacific Ocean at my back, and looking across at the Space Needle. It's a beautiful, hot, and sunny day. Running through downtown Seattle is anything but a pretty sight in the early morning. The scale of the homelessness and drug use is blatant at every corner. I slalom between the shadows sprawled out on the pavement, incoherent and lost, I'm eager to run out of the city jungle. Moving further east and across the Murrow Bridge, I relax in the more leafy and wealthy suburbs, leading out to the lakes area. The region has an air of a holiday resort, peppered with vast villas boasting views of lakes and rivers. Boats, kayaks, and paddle boards are orderly parked on pristine driveways.

I stop by Lake Sammamish, a splendid expanse of freshwater surrounded by a dense pine forest. Ariane, the Honorary French Consul, has invited me to spend the afternoon with her on the lake's banks, and go for a swim in its invigorating waters. I spot a few bald eagles, that majestic bird of prey that is the symbol of the country. I marvel at the wilderness of nature opening before me. Leaving behind the megalopolis, I sense the wild and natural state of the regions that I am about to explore. Ariane gives me a quick and informal safety briefing.

The reality of what I am about to attempt dawns on me. I'm going to cross the Rockies and some of its nature reserves. I am told to be on my guard. There are bears, cougars, and wild cats. I make a mental note that I need to find a bell to make noise, and bear spray, a sort of extra-sized tear gas. You do not want to catch these animals unaware. It's better to give them plenty of notice of your arrival, and failing that, ensure you have something to make them run away.

I remind myself of all the safety measures, no food in, or in close vicinity of, the tent when camping. A woman had been killed by a black bear in Montana earlier that month, having kept her food too close to her. I hear some stories from Ariane of goosebump-inducing attacks, where humans rarely have the upper hand. I don't let fear invade my thoughts, but I keep everything in the back of my mind.

I am more concerned with the heatwave situation. The whole northwest of the country is experiencing a record-breaking, hot summer, a climatic condition dubbed "the heat dome," with wildfires being the consequence of the extreme weather. I follow Ariane's advice and download an app onto my phone with the proper alert system to inform me of any fires close to my position. I do my very best to mitigate the risks by remaining cautious while keeping my mind free of worries. The immensity of the continent immediately strikes me. In Europe, which is so densely populated, I could easily find a town every forty kilometers or so. Upon leaving Seattle,

I contemplate a full 3,000-kilometer stretch into the unknown, across the states of Washington, Idaho, Montana, and North Dakota before I'll have Minneapolis in my sights. In between is mostly unpopulated land, with a smattering of small towns and flyover cities. The big Midwest is opening up to me, and the numbers are dizzying. I feel tiny, moving along at a snail's pace on this continent, which seemingly stretches to infinity.

My stroller is weighed down with a two-gallon water container, as well as my camping gear. It makes me (and the stroller) work a lot harder in the first week on the road. I climb and descend the Snoqualmie Mountains of the Cascade Range, through the wilderness of the national park. I run on trails and dusty roads, surrounded by tall pine trees and greenery. Here and there, I cross paths with the Yakima River and the many lakes of the region.

I reach Ellensburg for my first rest day and decide that Bob has had enough. All his rivets have come loose, though I have replaced them several times. The frame has lost its rigidity, and I no longer trust it. I strike luck, finding a replacement stroller of the same make and brand in the local pawn shop. The bell has tolled, and Bob Number One finishes his 16,000-kilometer odyssey by the side of a garbage bin in the motel's parking lot. I usually have no attachments to material things, but I do feel a pang in my heart as I leave Bob behind—my trusty travel companion.

Despite my efforts, I don't find the ultra-powerful tear gas in any shop. I know I am in bear territory, and there are signs on the side of the road to remind me of it. I even spot some bear tracks on a trail running parallel to the road. I reassure myself, thinking that the noise made by my stroller on these uneven roads should be sufficient to alert any wild animal of my presence.

Thankfully, on my tenth day of running, I come across a couple of travelers who offer me their tear gas dispenser, fully charged. My nights of camping in the wild will be more peaceful! I attach it to the handlebar of my stroller and practice unsheathing it several times to have it well at hand. I imagine that it could also help me out in the event of a dangerous encounter, like the characters of a Western movie, going for their guns!

Upon leaving Ellensburg, a group of cyclists breezes past me on a hill. The three leading men overtake me at high speed. The fourth in the group, a woman, slows down near me and checks in. Then, with a big smile she says to me, "Okay, you're on to something, where are you heading with your stroller?"

This is how I meet Dr. Lisa Bliss, pioneering medical director, and 2007 winner of the Badwater Marathon, one of the toughest endurance races on the planet. The 217-kilometer ultramarathon links the Death Valley, the lowest point in the US, to the top of Mount Whitney, 2,530 meters above sea level.

I am in the presence of an extraordinary athlete. We stop and talk for over an hour. In 2007, during her race, she pushed a cart to transport all the water she needed, achieving complete self-sufficiency. The resemblance of my stroller caught her attention. We exchange stories about endurance running.

Lisa's findings are backed by science, whereas mine (based on my eighteen month journey to date) are purely experimental. She fills in the gaps. There are still so many things that baffle me on a wide variety of topics: nutrition, recovery, adaptation, hydration, and the mysteries of biomechanics. When we say goodbye, it feels like parting ways with an old acquaintance.

That evening, I set up camp at the foot of the Vantage Bridge on the Columbia River, which forms Lake Wanapum in its widest arm. I wander to the edge of the lake to freshen up a bit and take in the scenery. The shoreline takes on a dark purple and orange hue as the sun sets on the horizon. I could not have picked a better place to pitch my tent. That evening, after a frugal dinner of bread and canned food, I go to sleep with the beautiful images and memories of the day, before waking up to the sound of birds singing all around me.

Lisa has arranged to meet me at dawn. She wants to shelter me with her car across the two-kilometer bridge, which she considers dangerous. She joins me at dawn and drives alongside me, hazard lights activated. There is, indeed, no space at all for pedestrians or cyclists, and I feel lucky to be the recipient of such attention. She then parks her car and takes her bike out of the trunk.

"I'll just ride with you for a little bit." She ends up cycling the whole way to Quincy, a full marathon under the blazing sun! Halfway there, we take a break at a deserted petrol station. She offers me bottles of iced water, which had been frozen overnight, and refills my snack reserves. Sitting in the shade of a parasol, Lisa tells me her story.

Lisa had been a very troubled teenager, and her life was turned around by a chance meeting with a teacher who helped her regain her confidence and made her return to school. She, too, was unable to have children. We have this in common, as well as a deep love for animals. We share our experiences, how the inability of creating a family had powerfully influenced the course of our lives. During our conversation, we are interrupted by my phone, which starts to vibrate.

My mother, worried about not seeing the point of my satellite beacon move, asks me why I am stuck at a petrol station, and wonders if I am safe! I am amazed by the precision of the satellite coordinates. I take a selfie with Lisa and tell her not to worry about me. I'm in good company on this vast continent, and I am being looked after.

I follow the canyons on peaceful roads devoid of traffic, the Grand Coulee in particular. The morning light gives the limestone an ever-changing face, in hues of dark blue, green, and grey, progressively changing to fiery colors, reflecting the rising temperatures as the cool morning slowly turns into an inferno.

These impressive limestone formations that stand in the hollows of the deserted valleys, as if sculpted on the banks of the rivers, paint the mood and emotion of the scenery. I am running in a live piece of art where every shade, every shape, is so precious and unique. The wild, harsh, and arid beauty of the landscapes touches me to the heart. Everything is new to me here. Mesmerizing.

I get acquainted with the prairie dogs, a type of small and vivacious marmot-like animal that appears in pastures, camouflaged by its light brown, sandy coat. They play hide-and-seek with me. I take some long breaks to observe them, spread out in the vast fields bordering the road. As soon as I hear one whistling and get ready to photograph it, it disappears, as if by magic. Another one pops up out of another tunnel to whistle in my direction. They seem to play a life-size game of whack-a-mole with me, and I willingly accept being the victim of their facetious ways.

As a backdrop to my footsteps, the immense sky of intense blue hangs aloft, unobstructed by any city or buildings. I am alone. I appreciate the silence, interspersed with the regular passage of enormous mobile homes, closer to a bus than to a caravan, towing cars, boats, and other leisure accessories. And then they disappear into the distance, swallowed by the illusion of the melting bitumen blurring the air on its surface. The soles of my shoes soften on contact with it, and gravel sticks to the melted rubber, sometimes making my strides awkward.

Step by step, I get deeper into another America. The one I knew was limited to a few business trips to New York and a road trip along the California coast. Knowing only of dense urban areas, business districts with dizzying architecture, skyscrapers, and a cosmopolitan atmosphere, the cliché of ultramodern and flashy megacities. But the vast underbelly of America reveals an entirely different identity.

I come across villages, and localities, whose isolation I feel. Everything is far away. The distances are a much bigger scale. I discover that water is often undrinkable, so I buy it in large plastic containers. The water sources are often polluted by agricultural and farming activities, as well as mining. And despite running in close vicinity to the beautiful wide rivers that crisscross the country, there is not a drop of potable water to be found.

In some of these regions, almost a third of the population lives below the poverty threshold. I stop by some settlements which boast very few activities outside the local saloon, the motel, or the petrol station. My wanderings take me past a ranch where the American flag flies high and proud. It's common in this country, where patriotism is openly expressed. Except this flag is hung upside down. In times of war, this sacrilegious gesture signifies that the country has passed into the hands of the enemy. In modern days, it signifies a strong opinion that elections have been rigged.

The 2020 presidential election is still viewed by many as a terrible injustice, and Trump supporters are making this known loudly.

At regular intervals, I also notice the presence of big billboards scattered by the side of the road. "Trump come back," "Make America Great Again," and "Trump President."

I understand that the defeat of the former president is still a painful and divisive subject in this land.

When I arrive in Coulee City, a town of 550 inhabitants, I check in at the local motel and head to the saloon, my new post-run routine. I sit on a bench to sip my beer while waiting for my burger and fries. By the counter, on a filthy table, an old man is leaning in front of his beer. He is thin, bony, with dusty grey skin. His dry white hair sticks out from under his wide-brimmed, black cowboy hat, and falls onto his shoulders. His beard is unkempt. Everything about the character gives the impression that he has been sitting there, in front of this beer, forever. Timeless, like everything in this bar, and in the city for that matter.

Without really moving, he stares at me for a moment, then speaks to me, "What are you doing here?"

I understand his surprise, as tourism is certainly not what keeps the local motel busy. The vision of a foreign woman alone is bound to raise questions. I cut to the point and tell him I'm running across his country. In a vain attempt to cheer him up, I add, "A bit like Forrest Gump!" His expression remains impassive.

"Like whom?" I don't show my surprise, and I move on with a remark about the day's run between the crushing heat, and the smoke from the surrounding fires. The old man asks me, "And where are you going tomorrow?"

"Wilbur, about fifty kilometers to the east." He makes a vague gesture, then nods his head, his eyes lost in the distance.

"Wilbur … I wonder what it looks like … never been there." America is not just a country of ultramodern nomads.

When I set out the next morning, the skies are a fiery shade of red. The air is hard to breathe, and a thick veil of smoke covers the valley. Wildfires are raging all around, and the air quality index is in the highly unhealthy range. People are encouraged to stay indoors. I decide to keep moving anyway and monitor, as best I can, all the signals that would indicate overexposure.

I draw on the experience of running in Singapore, through the fire season of Malaysian and Indonesian palm groves. I manage to run through the smoke and am surprised to receive so much support and concern from the locals. On this long ribbon of asphalt, meandering through the dried grass-covered rolling hills, I make progress under the watchful eyes of the sparse drivers I meet. People stop their cars by my side to ask if I need water, to check on me.

Weeks later, as I pitch my tent on some common ground, my phone alert suddenly rings. The whole area is under evacuation. What am I supposed to do? I run to the local gas station and, a little panicky, explain my predicament to the attendant. He plays down the whole situation, and a few locals around join him in reassuring me. They are all aware that I am camping on the field and assure me that no one will leave me behind if the situation becomes critical. I feel their concern for me, and though I don't know them, my instinct tells me to trust them. Despite the harsh conditions, I am touched by how hospitable and caring people are to me.

I run along the frontage roads, service roads parallel to the Interstates, or sometimes on country roads or trails when I find some. When none of these options are available, I run on the highways, which offer me a large and safe shoulder to run on. I'm protected from traffic not only by a line of yellow paint, but also by these tire-track marks that I have not seen anywhere else before. They are dug deep into the tarmac and would warn any vehicle drifting too close to the right to recenter. I feel safe, and I run unhindered. The only downside of running in the safety lane is the number of blown truck tires, which leave little metallic filaments scattered on the road. They have an appetite for sticking into my stroller's wheels, and I go through a fairly high number of punctures.

Traffic is light in the Midwest. The lighter it gets, the more people I meet on my adventure. My daily blog soon resembles a gallery of "the people of Montana," depicting new stories every day with happy smiling faces, giving my journey another dimension. A stark contrast to Europe, where (being so close to cities all the time) I was almost invisible. In these desolate landscapes, I stand out, and far from attracting the wrong crowd, I feel the kindness and support of those with whom I cross paths.

13

MONTANA ADVENTURES

The itinerary that I prepared at the last minute retraces at every point (although in the opposite direction) Steinbeck's journey in his story, *Travels with Charley*. It was not intentional, and it triggered all sorts of magical evocations of the names of certain states. Montana, North Dakota, and its thousands of kilometers of straight line, Minnesota, and Indiana, are names that had made me daydream as a teenager. I became conscious of the reason for this powerful appeal to the imagination. Thirty years have passed since I read the book, but Steinbeck's places and descriptions have remained intact, etched in my mind, invoking a return to the state of wonder he had plunged me into back then.

The words of Steinbeck resonate in my mind, "I am in love with Montana. For other states, I have admiration, respect, recognition, even some affection, but with Montana, it is love."

I run across the state, eager for it to reveal its secrets and work its magic on me. Interstates 90 and 94 will take me through the state via Missoula, Helena, Bozeman, Billings, and Miles City. Will I, too, marvel at these places? Will I be touched by their grace? More than sixty years have passed since Steinbeck traveled there. I wonder what will be left of these towns.

I also partly retrace the route of Lewis and Clark, the first explorers who crossed America from 1804 to 1806. Historical markers are spread on the roads and trails. I spot them regularly along the Columbia, Yellowstone, Missouri, and Mississippi rivers, recounting the advances of these pioneers. Their expedition not only made it possible to map the country but also to establish contact with the ancestral populations, the Native Americans. Unfortunately, this will mark the starting point of the colonization of these peoples. The pioneers had the promised land of the West in sight and conquered it with disastrous human consequences.

Montana is home to several Native American reservations: Flathead, Crow, and Northern Cheyenne. My route takes me near but not through them. In the heart of Montana, I cross the site of the "Sitting Bull Council," where the Duwamish and Suquamish Chief refused to sign the peace treaty but agreed to the movement of pioneers on these lands.

I stop for a long break. As far as the eye can see, I feel the timeless permanence of the beauty of the places that extend under the canopy of this immense sky. Exposed to the elements and harsh, untamed climatic conditions, the sprawling pastures are lulled by the song of sparrows and meadowlarks. I feel transported. Nothing has changed. I would not be surprised if an Indian emerged on horseback from the depths of this valley.

I am reminded of the speech attributed to Chief Seattle in 1854,

"How can you buy or sell the sky, the warmth of the earth? The idea seems strange to us. If we do not own the freshness of the air and the shimmer of the water, how can you buy them? Every piece of this land is sacred to my people. Every gleaming pine needle, every sandy shore, every shred of mist in the dark woods, every clearing and every insect buzz is sacred in the memory and experience of my people. [...] We know at least this: the earth does not belong to man; man belongs to the earth. We know this. All things are held together like the blood that unites the same family. All things hold together."[1]

He talks about the earth, rivers, trees, wildlife, and the precious, natural, cultural, spiritual, and transcendental balance between man and his environment. This land was not for sale.

I run along the railroad tracks that cross the country, another legacy of the early pioneers. On either side, cultivated fields form their typical circular shape. Livestock grazing on dry and brown grasslands stretch the horizon. When I happen to cross the course of a river, I run through the canyons, the valleys, and dense pine tree forests.

Montana offers a stunning and varied background to my journey. My routine consists of following the tracks for around fifty kilometers from village to village, station to station, and silo to silo. The population density is amongst the lowest in the country, and I come across more cattle than humans. From time to time, a car stops and people check on me, warning me of dangerous bushfires

1 "Chief Seattle's Letter to All," California State University, Northridge, http://www.csun.edu/~vcpsy00h/seattle.htm.

or a closed road. They ask if I need anything. A lone runner, stroller in hand, in the middle of these tremendous desolate expanses is certainly not an ordinary sight.

I often think of my great-grandfather, the father of my beloved grandmother. He was among the wave of Italian immigrants at the beginning of the twentieth century. I have never known him, and it is mainly through my father's recollections that I imagined what his life had been like. He arrived by boat via Ellis Island, then went to California, where he worked in a variety of jobs: railroad engineer, ranch boy, cartoonist, and banker. A resourceful and adventurous jack-of-all-trades. He stayed on the continent for around ten years before returning to Ascona.

I reminisce about this while running. I have often fantasized about what this adventure would have been like for him. I let the questions come to me. What had he come to look for? What did he find on these lands among all these uprooted immigrants who, like him, left everything for this continent? Was it the promise of a better life when Italy was experiencing dark times, between poverty and famine, as Fante himself describes it through Arturo Bandini, a product of this immigration?

But my great-grandfather came from the less affected Italian Switzerland, where he lived quite a comfortable life. What then? Just a little adventure? Was it the jitters that Steinbeck spoke of and that I recognized in myself? I will never have the answers to these questions. But on this American land that I travel on foot, I imagine what he must have experienced. Crossing the continent from the East Coast to the West by train, he must have felt all its immensity and beauty, seen the endless and almost virgin territories at a time when everything was yet to be built.

I travel alone and on foot in this mythical, distant continent, feeling its powerful appeal to the imagination. I push my house on wheels, chasing history, a trail of stories, and my story. It is through the effort, through my feet and my five senses, that this continent comes to life and reveals itself. I learn about its people, its richness, and its complexity.

Traveling solo in such isolated places can also be daunting. At the beginning of my journey through the continent, I gave myself an unnecessary fright. The day I reached Clinton, Montana, I found that the only available lodging option was an isolated lodge tucked between Interstate 90 and the Clark Fork River, ten kilometers east of the town. The region is of stunning natural beauty and wilderness, boasting lush pine forests, evoking the movie *A River Runs Through It*, which was shot there. It is a paradise for fly fishing and a prime ground for rainbow trout, attracting a niche public of wildlife aficionados.

I chatted with the owner of the lodge while devouring my regular lunch of a burger and fries. She took me to my room. The only one available was a little run-down hole. The whole lodge was being refurbished, and the place looked like a right mess. But I figured I would get a more comfortable night's rest here than in my tent. I settled for a nap and woke up to find there was no internet or phone coverage in the room. I went back downstairs to write my daily blog at the bar.

By mid-afternoon, the saloon was full of leather-clad bikers looking like easy riders. Long-haired, tattooed, loud, and downing beers like it was water. I was the only woman and non-biker customer around, and I caught them regularly glancing in my direction.

A little later, the owner came back to tell me the pub would close soon, and she would be heading back to her home in Clinton.

I'd be alone at the lodge and could call her if I needed anything. I wondered how I would do that since there was no phone signal in the room. Then, just before she left, she informed me the bikers had drunk too much to hit the road that night. They'd be camping on the lawn.

Right, so I was alone upstairs without phone or internet coverage. The nearest place was ten kilometers away, and there was a group of drunk men camping downstairs. Oh, and they had access to my bathroom since the bar's toilets were closed at night. On the one hand, I felt my fear was ridiculous. After all, I had been camping in the wilderness in total isolation. I have run thousands of kilometers on empty roads with no villages or inhabitants around. But there is something about drunken men and being the only woman with no access to communication that frightened me.

I didn't sleep much that night. I was on high alert every minute, clinging to my bear spray bottle and ready to draw at any time. As soon as the sun began to rise, I assembled my gear and ran out of it as quickly as I could. I hadn't eaten dinner the night before, hadn't had breakfast in the morning, nor had anything to drink. I hadn't refilled my bottles either and only had about one liter of water with me. Fear had gotten the worse of me.

Of course, everything backfired in style halfway through the run. The heat got to me. My throat and mouth were dry, burning with each breath of the scorching air. I rationed my water. When I could not take it any longer, I stopped by the side of the road, exhausted and desperately low on fluids.

I sat in the little shade offered by my stroller and waited. I realized how precarious my balance was. I rely on a good night's sleep, proper food, and hydration to get back on the road every morning.

When that balance is disturbed, things can turn sour quickly. Again, I was astounded by the generosity and hospitality from the people of Montana. Several of them stopped their cars to ask if I was all right and offered me water and food. I accepted eagerly, and their support was all I needed to get me to my next stage safely.

I am amazed at how easy it is to connect with people amid the isolation of the place. In a way, I answer their curiosity, and, in return, they'd tell me a bit of their story. I learned about the places I'd cross and a variety of topics. From town to town, saloon to saloon, I saw familiar faces. The owners of the taverns would often come to inform me that I had been expected. Word of mouth works its magic. Total strangers sometimes paid for my drinks and food. I experienced more encounters, heard more stories, and made more memories.

On days when I am camping, I feel the protection and care of my neighbors. They are keen to help me, offer me access to their electricity point, and share their food or drinks with me as an excuse for a chat and exchanging stories. I discover the world of the grey nomads, usually retired couples, who hit the road and live in their houses on wheels, free to go and set up camp where they please. I see them on the road sometimes. They recognize me, honk their horn, or stop for a chat and to offer a little encouragement.

I also notice how my fundraising for WFWI is taking off. Many of my new acquaintances hand me cash in hand after hearing of my fundraising efforts. This is something I hadn't seen in Europe, where people are more cash shy. Most importantly, I feel supported and encouraged. I gain the confidence I need to increase the distances and run much longer stages, going through fifty-kilometer stages two to three times a week.

Throughout the crossing of Montana, I also became aware of a new danger, a real and tangible one this time. I spot on the side of the roads and trails amusing words of warning on the portals, which often welcome the stranger with, "Prayer gets you closer to God. Trespassing gets you there faster!" Sometimes, they are decorated with intertwined pistols or skulls to clarify the message. I take note that I must not cross these high gates under any circumstances.

I follow the trails as much as possible to avoid running directly on the Interstate that leads to Bozeman, my stopover city for the day. I run, totally absorbed by my environment. The pine forest and the coolness of the river below offer me a welcome respite from the ambient heat. Lulled by the song of birds, in the serenity of the place, I am on autopilot, and I unfold my strides to the rhythm of nature without any worry in the world. I spot some wooden chalets on the side of the path, a few meters on. A man I hadn't seen turns towards me, blocking my way.

He faces me darkly. I'd disrupted him as he was loading the trunk of his car. The sound of my gear had startled him. He is shorter than me, plump, with his head devoured by large, thick glasses, giving him a mean and piercing gaze. He screams at me, "What are you doing here?" I don't immediately measure the level of his irritation.

"I'm running. I'm on my way to Bozeman," I reply.

His cheeks turn purple. He gets agitated and blurts out in one breath, "This can't keep happening. This isn't the first time. Can't you read? You're trespassing!"

The word sends shivers down my spine. I freeze and eye him more carefully. He has a rifle in each hand, and he is loading his trunk with hunting equipment. I have never seen so many guns in my entire life.

In a flash, I remember the signs on the portals, the skulls, and the guns. In Montana, private property is sacred. The law protects it against all odds. If that angry little man decides to shoot at me, he probably won't even have to justify self-defense. I know, damn it, it's written in the Second Amendment of the Constitution. Montana boasts the "Stand Your Ground" law, which is not very favorable to the trespasser, to say the least.

Before panic completely overtakes me, I throw my hands up in the air and repeat over and over that I'm sorry, that I didn't see the signs. My heart is racing. I'm struggling to breathe. My thoughts are blocked. I maneuver my stroller with one hand as best I can and turn around, then run away at full speed. Fear takes complete control of me as I race towards the Interstate.

My legs are still shaking when I reach the main road. This experience will not tarnish the rest of my journey with fear. It was my fault. Without realizing, I had passed signs indicating the start of private property. I expected it to be protected by a fence, a wall, or one of those big gates. But it was just a simple little sign placed at the side of the path. It's a lesson. Over here, men protect what's theirs with weapons. I will have to be extra careful. But if I run where I am allowed and pay attention, I know that I risk nothing. I continue my journey across North America, free and serene.

Through the crossing of Montana, I have managed to confront and overcome all the fears I anticipated at the start of this North American journey. Conquering my fear of the bears and other wildlife, fear of wildfires and the heatwave, fear of isolation, the local culture, and guns. It took a few brushes with them to free me.

The welcoming ways of the Montana people have won my heart, offering me an unforgettable experience and treasured memories.

I also feel strongly that my stroller, Bob, has played a prominent role in keeping me safe. Would this short-sighted, angry man have hesitated to use his guns if I had been running without a stroller?

14

A FEW WORDS ABOUT BOB

Summer is drawing to the end as I enter North Dakota. I like these border crossings, where the traveler is generally greeted by the state slogan. And after 1,200 kilometers through Montana, I am curious to discover another state. Here, I am welcomed with a huge sign urging me to "Be legendary!" I'm still smiling at the thought when I see a police car with flashing lights parking 200 meters in front of me on the emergency lane. A tall figure emerges, dressed in the typical brown uniform, pistol at the belt, cowboy hat screwed on the head, and radio in hand. It's the local Sheriff.

"I got calls from the central office about a woman running with her baby on the motorway. Does that ring a bell? Your ID, please."

I flash him a wide, toothy smile and open the stroller cover to take my passport out of the bag. The cop looks perplexed. He freezes for a moment. I tell him about the world run, hand him my business card, and to complete the picture, show him a preview of the journey's website on my phone. He takes off his sunglasses as if to gauge me better. His face changes expression, "You're a celebrity then? Can I take a photo with you?"

I'm not a celebrity, but the situation is now in my favor, and I don't contradict him. I comply and pose for the selfie. It will make a great story to tell his colleagues. He shakes my hand and stays behind me for a long while as I get back on the road. He finally hits the gas, "Bye-bye, Sheriff Corbyn!"

There is general confusion when people see me running with the stroller. They invariably mistake me for a mother jogging with her baby. I have met countless runners who, crossing my path, send tender glances in the direction of my equipment. They even encourage it. It will make the child a great athlete! I don't deny or correct them. I don't have time. And this misunderstanding amuses me. It's one more reminder that things are never quite as we imagine.

I am also not insensitive to the irony of the situation. I run, stroller in hand, painting the perfect image of the sporty mother who takes her baby out for a run. I, who was unable to have children, and owes my run around the world to not having any. Like many women, I grew up unconsciously projecting myself into motherhood. Whether we like it or not, the body is made for it, and the colloquial "biological clock" catches up with most of us at some point.

I got married at thirty. Five years followed, where I tried everything to get pregnant. I was monitored by specialist doctors and ended up resorting to painful rounds of IVF. These were difficult years. I was active and in great shape at the time. The doctors did not diagnose me with any abnormality or pathology.

Yet, I subscribed to the absurdity of sticking needles in my stomach three times a day, undergoing surgeries under general anesthesia while being completely healthy. The violence of the

My first marathon – *Athens, Greece – November 2004*

Start of the world run – *Cabo da Roca, Portugal – December 2019*

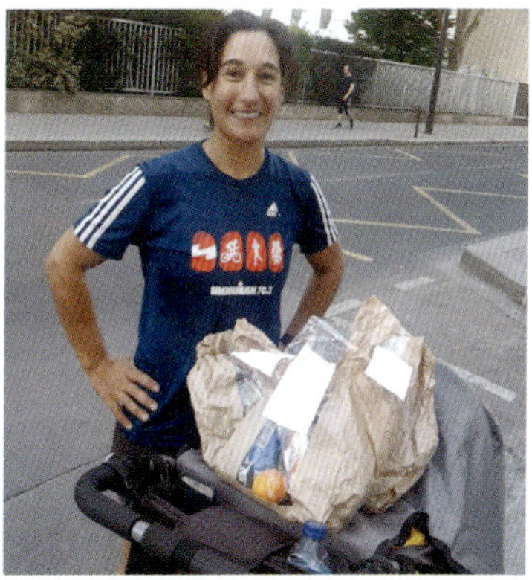

Distributing meals during lockdown – *Paris, France – April 2020*

Cooling down during the heatwave – *Lefkada, Greece – August 2020*

By the windmills of Peloponnese – *Tyros, Greece – August 2020*

Company on the road – *Thiva, Greece – September 2020*

Through the Balkans in the rain – *Maribor, Slovenia – November 2020*

Memorable welcome on New Year's Eve – *Chateaudun, France – December 2020*

Crossing the Ardennes under the snow – *Bastogne, Belgium – February 2021*

Running with friends in Switzerland – *Lausanne, Switzerland – March 2021*

Finish of the first continent after 15,000 km of running – *Istanbul, Turkey – June 2021*

Out of Seattle, sharing the road with trucks – *Vantage, USA – July 2021*

Warm welcome in the saloons of Montana – *Hysham, USA – August 2021*

With 77-year-old Gunhild Swanson – *Spokane, USA – July 2021*

Camping in the wild – *USA – 2021*

Entering North Dakota – *Medora, USA – August 2021*

Chicago Marathon finish picture – *Chicago, USA – October 2021*

Central Park with my parents – *New York, USA – November 2021*

Running through beautiful Mapuche territory – *Chile – December 2021*

With James, two on the road – *Chile – December 2021*

Stunning Lake District – *Chile – January 2022*

Shoe shopping by the roadside – *Chile – January 2022*

Andes, let the ascent begin – *Chile – January 2022*

A favourite of ours, evening barbecue – *Chile – January 2022*

Up the dirt trail – *Chile – January 2022*

Summit celebratory shot – *Chile – January 2022*

Descent on the Argentina side – *Argentina – February 2022*

Mafalda in San Martin – *Chile – February 2022*

Wild horses – *Argentina – February 2022*

Cooked by heat and humidity in the Pampas – *Argentina – March 2022*

Buenos Aires joyful arrival – *Argentina – March 2022*

Beware Kangaroos ... and flies – *Australia – May 2022*

Interesting read in Kalgoorlie – *Australia – May 2022*

By the fire in the Nullarbor – *Australia – June 2022*

A rescued joey near Cocklebiddy – *Australia – June 2022*

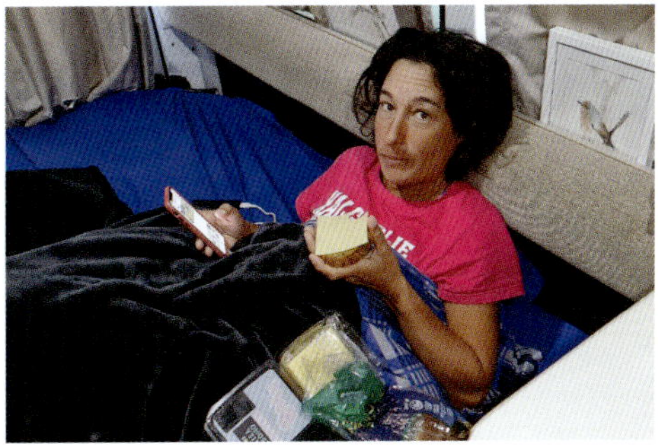

Breakfast in the motorhome – *Australia – June 2022*

Kimba, halfway through the continent – *Australia – July 2022*

My traveling companion, James, on his bike – *Australia – July 2022*

Post-run chilling in the motorhome – *Australia – July 2022*

Feeding a kangaroo in Adelaide – *Australia – July 2022*

Arrival in Sydney – *Australia – August 2022*

Finish picture with my parents – *Australia – August 2022*

Finish picture with James – *Australia – August 2022*

Meeting Rosie in England, post-world run – *Brighton, UK – April 2024*

procedures hit me hard. My body no longer belonged to me. Medicine had taken over. For something that seemed experimental to me, seemingly bordering on witchcraft.

Despite all my attempts over the years, it did not work. My world fell apart. As if the one universal thing that any woman in the world can aspire to do, regardless of her background, environment, education, or her aptitude for motherhood, was forbidden to me. I felt left out. Inadequate.

Desperately sad, I felt excluded from the playing field. Can a woman have a fully fulfilled life without going through motherhood? I didn't know because, at that point in my life, I had never asked myself the question. I felt lost with no answers beyond the incomprehension and the pain. I tried to understand why and what this intrinsic need was.

I understand that motherhood is something that is anchored in oneself since childhood in a logical, unique, and almost universal model, which has the advantage of answering many questions. What are we doing here on earth? I am not implying that giving birth magically answers anything. But by giving birth to another generation, each time expanding the field of possibilities and knowledge with scientific advances and philosophical reflections, and by improving the conditions of life on earth, our species may find the answers to the big questions of our presence here. Or not. It's a bit naive, I agree. But by being part of this march of humanity, reproduction, transmission, and progress, we give ourselves the hope of contributing to something much bigger than ourselves. To give life.

Beyond the need to reproduce, I also feel the desire to create a home. Life within a family is the only model I know. Even if I emancipated myself by leaving, alone and young, heading abroad for a nomadic existence, I no less wanted to lay the foundations of family stability. I wanted to center my world around the love for children, to know the simple joys of watching them grow, to accompany and guide little beings for whom we are infinitely responsible. I wanted to be present, take an interest in them, listen to them, value and love them, let them surprise me. The recipe seemed simple, but I knew that the path was also a complicated one. It was a path that I always knew I would choose, taking my life to a turning point that I was impatiently anticipating.

The shock of the closed door was devastating. It is often through the most difficult events in life that everything you take for granted gets challenged. The failure and ensuing grief resulted in divorce.

What followed was a questioning that lasted for several of my Singaporean years. I went as far away from home as I could, to Southeast Asia, halfway around the world, as if I had to be lost in every way to hope to find myself again. While continuing my practice of sports and running, I often succumbed to over-drinking at dinner parties or out in the town. Probably a way to forget that wherever I went, I was, and would forever be, a childless woman.

My friends all had children. They exchanged stories over dinner and at parties. This told me, with full force, the enormity of what I was missing. I was grieving. I went through the ups and downs, and my self-esteem was at rock bottom. I had nothing to offer anyone. At thirty-five years old, I was a second-hand, broken item. This is how I saw myself: divorced, childless, and unable to give birth. I lived from day to day without purpose.

I absorbed myself in work, sporting events, races, triathlons, and the annual Ironman that punctuated each season. I found a rhythm, if not a vocation. I pondered this additional irony. Through sport, I discovered treasures of unsuspected physical resources coming from my body, which was yet incapable of responding to its most basic and essential function of reproduction. They had a bittersweet flavor, these endurance races that I completed one after the other. I had to accept something from my body that I could not comprehend, that medicine could not explain. It had its share of mystery. In its refusal to comply, it pushed me to give meaning to my life in a different way.

This idea of a world run was the project I had been waiting for. Beyond the exceptional adventure and experience of the world, also emerged the beginning of my acceptance. I will be able to turn the page. Build other dreams. And over time, put to the test a quality that I had thought would only develop naturally through motherhood: going all the way and with complete dedication to the service of something beyond me—the famous responsibility of the parent.

I always anticipated that becoming a parent would bring a non-negotiable responsibility that I could not escape: every day, every moment, until the end of my life. From the moment I would have become aware of this life developing within me, there would be no escape, whatever the weather or the mood. But in the absence of children, I needed to accept that I would never know what it meant to carry the responsibility of someone other than myself for the rest of my life. I saw in this immense world run project, challenging the limits of what people believe to be possible, the possibility of an absolute commitment.

I transformed this quest for the world, which I had been pursuing for twenty years, into a quest for meaning. A chance to rediscover myself as a woman. Without children. A chance to take full responsibility and accept what my body imposed on me and the consequences for the rest of my life. This position in which I found myself must be my strength. I must use it to support the cause of other women. Show that we, too, can accomplish extraordinary things: be adventurers, explorers, and long-distance athletes. My grandmother worked in her library, patiently and for several decades, to honor the work of women in literature and give them the place they deserved. I am going to give myself the means to place yet another woman in the field of ultra-endurance, adventure, and exploration. I will share and inspire.

When, during my preparation in Australia, I tested the stroller solution to transport my equipment, and I understood the crucial role that it would play in ensuring my safety, I saw it as one more irony of fate. If this stroller, and the confusion it generated, turned out to be my greatest ally, my guarantee for a journey without bad encounters, without fear and with a free heart, then, so be it!

15

THROUGH THE GREAT PLAINS

At the end of summer, as I run along Interstate 94 between Medora and Belfield, I come across a stunning natural site, the Painted Canyons of Roosevelt Park. The name alludes to the lights, the changing colors, and the deep, dizzying canyons populated by bison, mule, deer, and wild horses. I take a detour to get a good look and sit on the rim, contemplating the prairie and the wildlife that strives amongst the juniper and wildflowers. I see the bison in their natural environment for the first time in my life. I am struck with emotion. These animals were relentlessly slaughtered by the pioneers, preferring the presence of domesticated cattle on their land. There are very few free-roaming bison left in the US. I measure my privilege to be able to watch them.

I am in the Badlands now, whose harshness Springsteen sings about. These arid lands are where nothing good grows and where life is brutal. I am touched by their beauty. They are a living piece of art, as the canyons and hills are slowly but constantly eroded by the hard rains. One day, these lands will be flat. It is hard to picture. I run through the dream, the folklore amongst the immensity of the landscapes that transport me. The music pulses in my head, giving my strides a boost of energy. When I arrive in Belfield, I stop for lunch at the local saloon adjacent to the motel. I see a lot of people around, and it's a welcome change for me. The canyons are the local attraction, and for several days, I have observed the increased frequency of mobile homes on the road.

Sitting at a table, eating my steak and fries, I sip an IPA, which is now my favorite beer. With my computer open and GPS connected, I'm writing my blog while all the adventures and discoveries of my morning marathon are still fresh in my mind. The stroller is parked beside me. I am still in my running gear. A woman in her sixties, sitting with her husband, suddenly gets up, pulls out the chair in front of me, and sits down. She plants her elbows on the table, locking her eyes onto mine and asks me point blank, "Are you on a mission?"

I stammer a semblance of a response, "A mission, I'm not sure ... What do you mean?"

She and her husband are visiting the national park. They have been traveling the road in their mobile home for the past three days, and they have seen me running with the stroller, sometimes in torrential rain, sometimes under the blazing sun, at distances that she considers extreme, every day. I laugh with the woman at her amazement and explain the world run.

Jan and Gerald have daughters my age, who now live far from home. One of them is a runner, and Jan tells me how seeing me by the side of the road has made her think of her daughter. Jan asks me about my route across the country. I open my Excel spreadsheet and show her my screen to reveal all the next stages. She studies the file, and her face lights up, "Oh, you're going through Detroit Lake!"

She and her husband have a bungalow there and are on their way to stay there throughout September. I will be there in a couple of weeks. Jan scribbles her address and telephone number on my placemat and says, "As soon as you pass the town entrance sign, call me. We'll be waiting for you."

Before she leaves, she gives me a very warm hug. I finish my meal, elated by this encounter and how the road has an endless stream of surprises for me every day. I get up to pay, but at the checkout, they tell me, "The lady and her husband paid your bill."

I continue my route through Bismarck, the capital of North Dakota, and the crossing of the Missouri River in early September brings about radical changes. The weather turns cooler, and I am now running amongst the drift prairies. Everything is greener. Trees and forests give the landscape a new dimension. Colors seem darker and contrast stark.

Of all the extreme conditions I have encountered through my journey, ranging from snow, rain, extreme cold and heatwave, the element that gives me the most grief is wind. Running into a headwind while pushing my bulky, thirty-kilo stroller in front of me is one of the most disheartening of efforts. I've learned to regulate my body temperature in extreme heat and keep warm in the cold. But the wind is an invisible force I have not found a way to adapt to. It never reveals how strong it is or how it will intensify.

I fight with it all morning on the day I run to Dawson, North Dakota. On either side of the dusty road, I run as relentless winds batter the wetlands. The vegetation seems to have disappeared, laid horizontal by nature's invisible hand. I struggle all the way, bent in half behind my stroller, pushing it against the mighty gusts.

I make it to town exhausted and mentally crushed, eager to lie down and get a good rest. The owners welcome me and take me to one of these big red barns, typical of the region, which has been converted into a guesthouse. Just as I am about to settle down, they invite me for lunch. How could I refuse? I join them, and we meet the local Pastor, Marvin, who freelances for the local paper.

I answer their curiosity, particularly Marvin's, who has prepared a thorough interview. The discussion turns to the region I am running in. I tell them how my crossing of their country has completely won me over. Marvin and Keith give me an account of the difficulties they have lived through. They talk with nostalgia about North Dakota, the second most oil-producing state in the US, in-depth of a rapid decline. They blame political decisions, which have contributed to the closing of multiple oil rigs. The region once boasted the lowest unemployment rate in the US. Now, people struggle everywhere.

I understand where they are coming from. The locals have a difficult choice, and there isn't much of an alternative. I am touched by these people and their openness, but I cannot help but think about the corollary. What about the damages to the environment, the infrastructure and the declining standard of living brought about by the oil industry?

Marvin takes me for a tour of the area in his car. He shows me a host of places by the lakes that once were full of life and activity and are now completely run down. I empathize with them and think about them often as I continue my journey through North Dakota.

I head towards Fargo through a series of flat trails and country roads. The landscapes are changing again. I am now traveling through the marshes. The drift prairies have given way to lakes, the prairie dogs of the Badlands to wild ducks, and my run is accompanied by the croaking of frogs. I run absentmindedly on the side of the highway, already nostalgic about the big Midwest crossing coming to an end. But North Dakota has one more surprise in store for me.

A few days earlier, a local newspaper, *The Jamestown*, published an article about my world run, in which I appeared on the front page. The photo shows me in action, stroller in hand, my pink cap screwed on my head. Taking me out of my reverie, a black convertible coupé slams on the brakes, swerves to my left, and parks in front of me in the emergency lane. At the wheel is a blond woman, looking completely distraught. She gets out of the car and faces me with tears streaming down her cheeks. She sobs and falls into my arms.

Throughout her fragmented story, peppered with hiccups, I try to understand her upheaval. Today marks the first anniversary of her only son's death, who was murdered mysteriously, a cold case among many others. Pamela is crushed by grief, and this morning, she says she took the wheel, "to look for something, anything, a sign that life is worth living despite the pain." She'd been driving for hours, aimlessly. When she saw me along this road, she recognized my photo from the newspaper. My fantastic journey had made her dream yesterday, and this unexpected meeting was the sign she was waiting for.

I, in turn, am struck by the vivid and raw emotion of this woman, a mother and by the ray of light that my journey provides her. I take her in my arms and give her a warm hug to calm her sobs. She digs into her bag and pulls out a piece of fabric embroidered with her son's name and his dates of birth and death. She slips it into my hand and asks me to promise her to take with me around the world this symbol of the memory of her child.

I understand that through this simple gesture, she hopes to think of her son without the weight of mourning and sadness, to imagine him embarking on a beautiful journey with the pink-capped runner. I promise her that I will store the fabric carefully in the waterproof pouch where I keep what is most precious to me. My journey has provided us both with an improbable encounter, charged with an intensity that turns me upside down.

Two weeks later, I cross into Minnesota, the "Land of 10,000 Lakes." I am picked up on arrival by Jan and Gerald, perched on their golf carts on the banks of Detroit Lake. Jan hugs me and proceeds to load my belongings onto the buggy. She gives me a tour of the resort and takes me to their bungalow.

Neighbors start to flock, and we quickly find ourselves part of a big group at the barbecue Gerald is preparing. My hosts offer me a friendly, almost familial, break. I feel so grateful for all the opportunities this adventure is providing me, like a gift that keeps giving. We eat, drink, laugh, and talk as if we have known each other for years. As usual, the world run intrigues and sparks conversations. I listen to each other's stories, feats of arms and dreams. In the middle of the afternoon, they take me to visit the surroundings of the lake. I observe the hummingbirds on their migratory journey. It's the first time I've ever seen them. Everything is so beautiful and surreal.

Dinner is more intimate. Jan and her friends question me, trying to understand my state of mind, my motivation, and the source of my enthusiasm and energy. Gerald, a giant of almost two meters with a bear-like physique, participates in silence. I feel it; they look at me with a kind and protective intention. I am the age of their daughters, which might explain it.

I get up at dawn the next day. Jan and Gerald are already up in the kitchen, busy preparing me a breakfast of champions. At the door, they wait for me to start my GPS and satellite and close the stroller compartment. Jan hugs me again. She has tears in her eyes when she says, "I know you already have a mum, but I will follow you like one and worry about you until you arrive in New York. I will try to remain discreet and not send you too many messages."

All these experiences bring us closer together. They give the world its human dimension, familiarizing me with places, continents, and people across diverse and varied cultures. It is with the same humanity that all around the globe, we welcome the foreigner or the stranger, offering shelter and sharing bread with the traveler. I touch on something universal, a common denominator, and my journey seems to elicit the best in the people I meet.

But all good things come to an end, and I am now running towards a more densely populated area, with the Great Lakes and the Rust Belt looming ahead.

16

ACROSS THE RUST BELT

After 3,000 kilometers of running on the continent, my arrival in Minneapolis marks a turning point. Gone are the semi-desert immensities, the isolation and tranquility of the endless countryside. I'm getting closer to the East Coast. Oddly enough, I feel more vulnerable as I approach the urban jungle than when I crossed the country's Midwest.

The experience of reaching Minneapolis is a mixed one. On the one hand, I am excited to discover the city, marvel at the tall glass buildings, visit the department stores to buy new shoes and running gear and walk the streets amongst people going about their daily routines. Stopping by for a coffee and a snack, eating more varied foods, or spending the afternoon just wandering around and getting lost in the city. These things I haven't been able to do since leaving Europe.

On the other hand, I feel all the brutality of life in a big city. The sound gets to me first, with the traffic noise and sirens of police or emergency vehicles. Noise from construction sites and public works adds to the agitation. Then there is the indifference; everyone minding their own business, oblivious to anyone else.

The traffic lights and the pavements are so treacherous for a stroller! Stop and go, up and down the high steps with a thirty-kilo dead weight at my arms. Misplaced bins or litter discarded on the sidewalk obstruct my run. I feel for all those who have to navigate the busy streets with a "real" baby stroller or a wheelchair.

It's an abrupt reconnection to the real world. My timing coincides with the first year that has elapsed since the George Floyd controversy occurred. I find myself at the heart of current events and tensions between communities. Everywhere, signs proclaim people's solidarity with the Black Lives Matter movement, and police cars patrol the streets. It strikes me that I can't remember having seen a person of color since I left Seattle a few months earlier.

I enjoy a rest day in the city set by the mythical Mississippi River and try to embrace the new, more urban chapter of my crossing. From this megapolis to the next one, I will run through the countryside of Minnesota, Wisconsin, and Illinois. Autumn starts showing its true colors, painting the green countryside with beautiful touches of bright red, yellow, and brown. I am witnessing my first American indian summer with balmy temperatures along the Mississippi and Minnesota river trails. The terrain is flat. The air is pure and cool as I go through a few weeks of my fastest running throughout the journey, feeling healthy and robust.

I come across a string of middle-sized cities which offer me an exceedingly different experience. Hotels and motels are often located at the periphery of the towns, surrounded by commercial centers and food chains, such as Applebee's and all the classic fast-food brands. On the upside, my diet has become much more varied. My choice is no longer limited to burgers and fries versus the tasteless frozen Badlands pizzas. On the downside, I am on the outskirts of city life, no longer in the center of the community. On the roads and trails that I run every morning, I no longer stand out as the odd one. In other words, I blend in.

Reaching the center of big cities involves running across all the circles of their suburbs, one by one. The condition of the roads and front yards tells me something about the standard of living of the inhabitants. I discover the effects of gentrification, and impoverishment through these successions of radically different communities and wealth. My arms are working at full capacity, maneuvering the thirty-kilo stroller on the broken sidewalks, getting it up and down and dealing with the incessant cuts in pedestrian spaces. I adapt and discover a new world. Leaving a big city is often followed by tens of kilometers through industrial zones before returning to the calm of the countryside or the lakes.

There is a rendezvous I am looking forward to honoring. To make it on time, I run an uninterrupted streak of fourteen days without a rest day. The meeting had been set up a couple of months earlier. When the French Consul of Istanbul contacted his network in the US to inform them of my journey. The Chicago team picked up the call. They got in touch with me with one idea in mind: participating in the famous Chicago Marathon. It is one of the six "World Majors," and is held in October. The event is even more exceptional this year, as it has not been organized for two years due to COVID restrictions.

Two months before the race, with my enthusiastic approval, they arrange to add me to the list of participants. There is one condition, though. I will have to abide by the rules. I am not allowed to run with my stroller. This is non-negotiable.

At dawn on October 10, 2021, I take the train from the western suburb of Chicago, where I ended my thirteenth consecutive marathon the day before. The carriages are full of runners and smell of muscle rub cream and suntan lotion. I take the short walk to the starting pens amongst the thousands of other runners. The atmosphere is quiet and friendly, full of expectation and nervousness. It is a far cry from the loneliness of my daily runs, where my breathing and footsteps are often the only noises that disrupt the surrounding quietness.

I line up alongside 30,000 other runners with a certain apprehension. Will I manage to run without my stroller, having covered almost 20,000 kilometers with it as an extension of my arms? I wonder! It's strange and yet joyful to set off amongst so many other runners. Strange, because I had forgotten that this distance had such a mythical connotation. For my part, I have completely normalized the exercise. It is joyful because sport is a celebration of life, health, and a great vector of connection between people and communities.

The nervousness of some and the excitement of others all take me back to my first racing experience. What a happy festival, what enthusiasm, what commitment on the part of all the communities of Chicago! I rejoice in the orchestras and bands placed along the route, the spectators dancing, singing, applauding, and holding up all kinds of signs to encourage the runners. The Chicago Marathon is a superb celebration, meandering through all the different neighborhoods of the city and worthy of the great carnivals.

I let myself be carried away by this festive atmosphere. My doubts fade. I run like a metronome at the rhythm that has been imprinted on my body for so long, four hours, thirty-four minutes split into two equal halves of two hours and seventeen minutes. This time, it's an official timing stamp that says so. I couldn't have been more consistent! It was amusing to notice how many runners passed me by in the first half of the run, so fast that I wondered if I had not taken off from the wrong Start Pen. Then, as we hit the thirty-kilometer mark, things turned around, and I started passing runners who seemed to have succumbed to the famous wall. I have always considered the "marathon wall" a construct that every runner is taught to fear. I don't think there is any basis for it other than psychological.

I suck in the atmosphere and the exceptional vibrancy as I approach the finish line. I let the volunteers place a medal around my neck and then pose for the traditional finish photo. I'm proud as punch and delighted to have been given the chance to partake in this fabulous and grand celebration.

The next day, I resume my running across the city and stop for a pit stop at the French School of Chicago. Dozens of children and their teachers accompany me on the last mile to the Lyceum. The school assembly, presided over by the dean and the consul, offers me a very warm welcome. I spend the next few hours in the schoolyard with the children, answering all their questions and curiosities. Some of them seem more impressed by the fact that I had run the Chicago marathon the day before, not realizing that I had already run the equivalent of five hundred marathons before I reached the starting line!

I wave a cheery farewell to Chicago, turn my back, and continue my route through the states of Indiana, Ohio, and Pennsylvania. In rural Indiana, running through the Amish County of Shipshewana, I share the road with horse carriages. The carts, made of a stern, big black box with a tiny window, look sober and solemn.

I spot some children peeking outside to have a good look at the runner with the baby stroller. They seem too shy to wave at me, but we look at each other with the same reciprocated awe! It's Sunday morning, but all the children are out and about on communal grounds in their black and white outfits. It's church day, and religion is deeply rooted at the center of the Amish culture.

This is also my first Halloween in North America, and I am amazed at how seriously the event is celebrated nationwide. In the weeks leading up to it, it seems every barn, farm, and house I run past is decorated with pumpkins, ghosts, witches and spiderwebs. There are even prizes for the best-decorated houses and towns, as well as the most haunted houses!

I run on my own, on secondary country roads or nature trails. Autumn has set in. The weather is colder and wetter. Nature is now more shaded in brown. I come across a bizarre sight the day I enter Pennsylvania. A drunken racoon! The poor animal is stuck in the middle of the road, moving erratically and seemingly lost or incapacitated. With the help of a local man, I try to guide him to the roadside. He's blocking traffic, and vehicles are starting to pile up. A police car shows up. The very unimpressed officer mutters something under his breath about "another drunk racoon."

He is amused at my surprise. These animals have a habit of eating fruit off the ground, which ferments while rotting for too long. The alcohol content increases and that's how the poor racoons become so disoriented.

Mid-November 2021, I finish my marathon symbolically at the entrance gate of the White House. I am greeted by around ten women from WFWI, whose headquarters happens to be in the American capital. For almost two years, I have been fundraising on their behalf, and I am delighted to have this opportunity to meet some members in person. They offer me handmade artefacts from some of the countries where women receive help rebuilding their communities and economies. It touches me deeply, and I hope that, in return, my epic voyage can show them that women are not limited in their endeavors nor their resources.

Another surprise awaits me. My parents have been able to fly to the US, just as the country has started reissuing travel authorizations for short-term stays. I smile at the vision of my mother and father in front of the Capitol with masks on their faces, suitcases in their hands, and rushing to hug me. This world run never ceases to offer me unpredictable and wonderful moments. The reunion is as joyful as it is unexpected! We set out for an afternoon of sightseeing. The setting of the capital, whose white buildings radiate under the powerful blue sky and the gentle autumn sun, gives this moment a solemnity and an emotion that takes me by surprise.

We are hosted by Victoria, an active supporter of women's rights and an influential community member. She and her husband Franklin, welcome the three of us into their family, making us feel at home and looked after. The next day, members of the community and the WFWI flock into the house to attend the afternoon buffet our hosts have organized. An occasion to share more about the journey and give a new boost to my fundraising efforts.

When I leave Washington, DC, I have ten days of running left to reach New York City. I am heading to the East Coast with a peculiar feeling, and I know I cannot miss this next meeting either. Something awaits me!

17

NEW YORK, SECOND CONTINENT CROSSED

From the capital city, I reach Baltimore on the East Coast, and I see the Atlantic Ocean before me. Four and a half months have passed since I left the Pacific Ocean on the West Coast of the Continent. The emotions I feel are overwhelming. Having traveled on foot has given me an acute impression of the land's enormity. My experience must not have been too far away from the first explorers, mapmakers, and pioneers. Not only do I grasp the distances, but I also feel the country's richness, greatness, and diversity. I try to keep my emotions under control as my run in North America is not over just yet. Technically, I could have chosen to finish my crossing here. But I thought, for many reasons, that a finish in New York City would be more meaningful.

From Baltimore, my running takes me through Philadelphia and New Jersey, from town to town and across the suburban countryside. I feel evermore like a grey traveler, the one no one notices. I push my stroller on busy streets, where busy people mind their own business and go about their day. I feel like shouting at the top of my voice, "Hey everyone, I've just run across your country, all the way from Seattle!" but I keep it inside. I'm boiling with impatience.

On the eve of my arrival in New York, I have another meeting with my parents, this time at Ellis Island. In the twentieth century, this small island was the main port of arrival for all immigrants in search of the promised land. It has a special meaning for us since it is here that my great-grandfather arrived around 1900 before moving to the West Coast to settle there. A family story that I largely idealized.

After a few years working on the Californian coast, Amedee Righetti, the father of my beloved grandmother, learned that he had inherited a ranch in Australia. He then crossed America again in hopes of boarding a liner en route for the Antipodes. Unfortunately, on the day of the departure, a striking picket line blocked all port activity in New York. My great-grandfather threw an Italian tantrum. A fight ensued, during which he fell into the water. He ended up being picked up on a liner en route to Europe! The end of his nomadic life and a one-way ticket to Ascona. He never got to see his Australian inheritance.

The bizarre and eccentric stories that circulate about my great-grandfather are part of our family folklore and have always tickled my imagination. I envied my father, who heard them as a child from the protagonist's mouth. It must have been fascinating even if the custodians of his stories were especially marked by the character's rough and moody demeanor.

The three of us set out to visit Ellis Island, this symbolic place of twentieth-century immigration. I let my parents try to trace the footsteps of our temperamental ancestor in the dedicated research room. We come out with a digital copy of his entry certificate. A small victory, even if some errors in the dates cast doubt on its authenticity. Regardless, I continue to walk (or rather run) in the footsteps of my family history with my parents by my side to celebrate this milestone of completing my second continental crossing.

The next day, I run my last North American marathon, rallying Jersey City to Manhattan via the George Washington Bridge. I start from the Waterfront, on the opposite shore of the Hudson, where the site of the World Trade Center stands. The air is crispy, clear, and cold, and the sky is intensely blue and bright. I keep glancing to my right. Manhattan cuts such a distinctive skyline. I make sure the American flag I bought yesterday is solidly attached to my handlebar. I make it up to the bridge, which boasts a wide pedestrian corridor, giving stunning views of the city from the north. From up here, I have a bird's-eye view of the island and the Hudson River. Central Park's green and brownish forest seems to take up the whole space. And in the distance, the famous cityscape is recognizable in an instant.

I reach Central Park directly from the bridge via the Riverside Trail. My heart is racing, and I recognize this powerful emotion brought about by the inevitable mini-assessment at the end of a continental crossing. Memories flock to mind in a messy jumble. I recall the pallet of colors that have painted my journey, the sunrises over the canyons, the valleys, lakes, and rolling hills. I remember the sensations and changes of the seasons, from the heatwave to the Indian summer, the sights and sounds of the birds and wildlife, as well as all the people I have met, their stories and the fears I left far behind. My head spins with memories!

A group of French runners await me inside Central Park and run by my side for the final few kilometers. They adorn my stroller with French flags, too. The mood is jovial. Some of them had run the New York Marathon several weeks earlier. I could not make that on time, though it would have made for a beautiful finish, too!

We finally exit the park and take a turn into Fifth Avenue. The consul and his staff, my parents, a representative for WFWI, and members of the French community are here to give me a warm welcome and celebrate with me. What a joy.

The arrival in New York marks two years of running, with 21,000 kilometers on the clock. I have traveled across sixteen European countries and fourteen North American states. My average speed of just over nine kilometers per hour has been consistent since the start. I feel healthy and as energized and fueled by desire as I was two years ago. I am also the happiest I have ever been, filled with purpose and positively driven.

We head upstairs, where the consul has prepared a reception. I don't often have time to share my reflections about the journey. My daily blog is more of a day-to-day account. But I now get to answer questions like, "What is the purpose of the journey?" "Why running?" and "What is your most powerful memory?"

These allow me to elaborate on the value of traveling slowly, on foot. These events are also the perfect occasion to boost my fundraising efforts.

The consul offers me accommodation in his mansion on Fifth Avenue, with a view of Central Park. Being received for a few days, with honors, allows me to put into perspective what I am currently on the path to doing. I often trivialize my adventure because it's my daily life. These continental arrivals are a reminder that I am on the road to a truly extraordinary quest.

I spend one last day with my parents, sightseeing around New York. Then comes the time to say goodbye. The third continent of my odyssey is waiting for me, and this will be my first crossing into the Southern Hemisphere.

18

IN COMES JAMES

With two years of running solo and over 21,000 kilometers under my belt, the journey is now well-established. I could continue like this until the end of the adventure, comfortably settled into my well-organized routines and my trail of endless discoveries. But a little revolution is brewing, which finds its source in the devastating fires of the summer of 2021.

When crossing Montana, I received a message from my friend Lisa in Greece, which took me down in the middle of a marathon, "James' house has just gone up in flames," it said.

I was stunned by the brutality contained in these few words. I carried on running, mentally scrolling through all the memories I have of this beautiful family home, built by James' parents in the 1970s when they left England to settle near the Hellenic capital. The house featured a vast garden planted with a jumble of trees, where birds and cicadas sang from morning to evening. A green paradise perched on the mountainside, at the heights of

Athens, sheltered by the surrounding pine forests, which gave it fresh air in the summer heat. A welcoming place where friends often met for the afternoon or evening, sometimes for the start of a hike, or bike ride.

I met James in 2007 as I took my first steps organizing triathlons in Greece. Lisa used to volunteer at the races, helping with aid stations or at the finish line. She also regularly invited her friends to participate. This is how James became familiar with triathlons and another friend in my circle. We share fifteen years of a dotted friendship, paced by my visits to Greece. When I learned of the fire in his house, I sent him a message to show my support. Cautious to conclude with a note of humor, I told him that one can live a very happy life with a small bag of clothes that fits in a "supermarket shopping cart." This is the term he used to describe my stroller.

James replied almost immediately, and from there on, our conversations began. We called each other at the end of my runs and talked, sometimes for hours. We got to know each other through our respective journeys, the state of mind with which we confronted, and dealt with, our struggles and difficulties. I became attached to our daily meetings and welcomed the change it pushed into my routines (making time for someone else). It also gave me a taste of what it would be like to have a travel companion. I realized how richer the journey and its events became once you could share them closely with one another and form common memories.

I recognized in James this quality of going alone to accomplish his most personal, most important projects without waiting for the conditions to be ideal because they never are. For fifteen years, he has run a business aimed at discovering a lesser-known Greece by bike. This is in addition to his day job as a maritime adjuster.

He spent his free time scouting itineraries and guiding mountain bikers on rugged trips well off the beaten path. Passionate about history and in love with this country, he has shared his most beautiful discoveries. When the migration crisis affected the Greek coastline in 2016, James was prompt to help with his boat long before the NGOs came to bring some order to the surrounding chaos. He stationed himself on Lesvos for several months and crisscrossed the sea, day and night, watching for wrecks that ran aground or capsized off the coast to aid and rescue migrants.

On one of our phone calls, I said to him, "Since you no longer have a house, possessions, or any immediate plans, why don't you come and join me in South America? You could help me cross an almighty mountain range!" I said it as a joke, but this invitation reflected a real need.

In the planning stage of the world run, I had identified two places where I could use assistance. The first would be the crossing of the Andes between Chile and Argentina, because climbing to an altitude of 4,000 meters with the thirty-kilo stroller seemed challenging to me. The second was the Nullarbor desert plain in Australia, where the distances between two stages can reach up to 200 kilometers, forcing me to carry all my water for five days of autonomy (an additional thirty kilos at least). To my surprise, I didn't even have to convince him. James accepted on the spot.

I had not imagined he would respond so quickly, with such certainty, and I sensed they were not empty words. Throughout the discussions that followed, James transformed the initial proposal.

"Since I am joining you for part of the journey in the mountains, why don't we cross the entire South American continent together?" he suggests. The die is cast.

We both took the time to reflect and adjust to each other. Every evening over the phone, we discussed and organized this adventure together. Every morning, during my four or five hours of running, I projected myself and questioned this new direction that I was about to take. I often heard runners talk about the monotony during long endurance runs. For my part, I never felt it. My daily marathons constitute a privileged space for reflection. It was already the case before James came into the picture. It had become more specific and a place to question the very essence of my commitment. The thought of this new direction concerned me.

I took the time to welcome my doubts and my fears, and to express them during our calls. I discovered that I am very protective of the characteristics of my journey. I love moving into the world in autonomy and self-sufficiency. It makes me free to appreciate the quality of the silences, be the sole master on board and drink the cup of total freedom to the dregs. I understood that I would have to let go of a few things, particularly the notion of time, which has been crucial in my considerations. I noticed it every time someone joined me on the road. Time finds its place. "Around what time do you think you'll arrive?" "What time do we meet for lunch or dinner?" "When do you want to leave?"

When alone, I am accountable to no one. I let the road, the elements, and the terrain, dictate my pace, without constraint. But all my doubts fell away one by one. When I worried about whether James might get bored with my slow pace, he replied, "I can spend a whole day being interested in a stone. Don't worry about me!"

I was taking another leap of faith. In this seemingly fragile and tailor-made endeavor, the balance of which seemed to depend on maintaining the organization and the routines I have put in place,

I decided to redistribute the cards. In a way, the framework had already been roughed up. If it had survived the hazards of a pandemic, it may well adapt to the addition of a travel companion! I let go of my worries, deciding it would be worth it.

At the end of August 2021, the revolution began. James would join me in Chile, at the start of the South American crossing. Quite an undertaking since we had never been alone together, having socialized only within a group of Lisa's friends!

We both had three months to prepare. It was an upheaval for James too. After his house went up in flames, he took refuge on an isolated peninsula on the island of Euboea, where there was another house, made of stone, that he had just finished building. On this arid land where nothing grows, he patiently created a garden where a multitude of trees fight against the elements. The winds there are the most powerful in Greece. Nothing can resist the gusts of more than 100 kilometers per hour, which can blow relentlessly from morning to evening, except for James' trees. He has three months to set up an irrigation system to ensure their survival in his absence.

He had to finish several cases he was working on and manage the aftermath of the fire, in which he lost everything, including his identity papers and passport. Not to mention the ballet of procedures to be undertaken with the insurance and other administrative tasks. Those three months would be a mad race against time for him in an already hectic period. Beyond the efforts he had been making, he was also mourning the house built by his parents, where three generations of his family had lived.

In the middle of this whirlwind, I began to imagine and put together the logistics for two. It slowly took shape, building the plan with James as a non-adjustable variable. He would travel by bike, but we decided to rent a minivan to transport our belongings. It would afford us the latitude to discover more of the regions we pass through.

The presence of a vehicle would allow me to rework my route without being dependent on stopover villages. This huge logistical constraint would be disappearing. I could consider finishing my run in the middle of nowhere once the day's mileage was reached. The van would allow me to travel back and forth between the finish point of the run and the village where we would spend the night.

I spent the necessary time working on the plan. James, for his part, was researching the part of South America that we will explore. He brought me a different perspective. I adapted my route plan according to his curiosity and ideas. I included the region of lakes and volcanoes at the gate to Patagonia, which we will cross before hitting the Chilean coast and, before our ascent over the Andes. I had no regrets about the way I had progressed so far, but I was discovering, with James by my side, a new form of freedom which would undoubtedly enrich my world run.

Time passed quickly for both of us. November 2021 was coming at full speed as we ironed out the final organizational details. When my North American crossing concludes, we decide to spend a week together before the big departure for the third continent, adjusting to each other and taking the time to breathe. My first world run holiday, although I often tell myself that this trip is, in fact, a vacation in itself!

When I leave New York for this week-long break in the sun, I know that I am ending the first part of my journey of two years traveling solo. I eagerly await for James to join me and breathe new life into the world run, to provoke changes bound to enhance my experiences. For the coming months, I will no longer move forward in the world alone on the roads, stroller in hand, without anyone to answer to. I will finally be able to share the most wonderful adventure of my life with a traveling companion.

19

SOUTH AMERICA, TWO ON THE ROAD

At dawn on December 12, 2021, I dip the wheels of my stroller in the Pacific Ocean, at the port of Maullín and the gates of the Chilean Patagonia. Though he doesn't have to, James symbolically rides his bike beside me in the same waters. Then, we turn inland towards Puerto Montt.

There is no reason I should be running with the stroller other than the fear of changing my well-oiled routine. The stroller is convenient, providing me with a little cockpit. On the handlebar are my two GPS devices, giving me information on kilometers and routes. In the front pocket, the satellite tracker flashes its green light and warns me when the batteries are running too low. On top of it, my two isotherm bottles containing 1.5 liters of water. In the bottom compartment, my rain gear, windproof jacket, and a warm top, which I use on my breaks or when it's chilly. On the first day in South America, I was not ready to make a compromise with my gear and my habits, running as I did before.

It doesn't take long to change my mind, though. We have chosen to avoid running on the Pan-American Highway, Ruta 5, which crosses the country from north to south. The route would have been my obvious choice if I had been alone, but being with James and having the minivan allows me to run on country roads in a more peaceful and natural environment. I don't have the constraint of going from town to town. Unfortunately, rural roads in this part of the country are unpaved and covered with a mix of loose stones and gravel. The first day with the stroller is difficult enough to convince me to pack it up, load it in the minivan, and learn to run with a few kilos on my back. Bob continues his journey in the back of the minivan.

My entire posture needs readjustment, from swinging my arms, to keeping my back straight. I place a towel around my neck to stop the backpack from rubbing and cutting into the flesh of my shoulders. My travel companion on three wheels has been retired, and there is no time to mourn it. In its place is James, riding his bike to meet me on the road with supplies of fresh water and treats. He has many qualities that Bob was lacking! He is particularly entertaining and supportive. James sometimes parks the van at the halfway point to brew a cup of tea or prepare a marmite toast, awaiting me with a camping chair and a poncho.

Our minivan is quite flamboyant. Its sides and back are decorated with colorful frescoes depicting the landmarks of Chile. It is adorned with images of araucaria trees, volcanoes, cacti, condors, a couple of llamas, a whale, and sea lions. Our "Condor Camper," as it is named, is equipped with a burning stove, a barbecue, and a reserve of fresh water. The inside can also be turned into a sleeping area, though most of the time, it is packed tight with the stroller, the bike, and our bags. We travel in style and certainly do not go unnoticed.

We meander through the Lake District and the volcanoes on this narrow stretch of Chile, wedged between the Andes and the Pacific Ocean. Though the mornings are quite cold, the air usually turns into a furnace by midday. I run on the rolling dusty hills, surrounded by a mix of dense forests and green fields of pasture. The volcano summits, covered in snow, cut majestic and imposing figures against the skies of bright and intense blue. Many of these are still active and casually release little rings of smoke at regular intervals.

My routine is drastically different. I no longer need to finish the run at the exact place I'm staying for the night. So, I stop when I have reached my target mileage (still set above forty kilometers a day). James ends his biking for the day, jumps into the van and meets me at the prearranged finish spot. From there, we drive to the nearest village or lodge. I enjoy the change and the novelties of the journey. We are now able to cook our meals wherever we are. I don't think any dinner will ever be as good as the ones we cook at dusk on the barbecue outside the little wooden cabanas that scatter the Chilean countryside, where we often stay. We sit under the stars, in nature, enjoying the freshness of the evening air.

Chile's Lake District is stunning and welcoming. At the foot of the snow-capped volcanoes, water gathers in glacial blue lakes before draining via the main rivers to the Pacific Ocean. It is difficult to resist going for a swim in such scenery, however cold the water is. We wiggle our toes into the soft black sand, warm from the volcanic activity. This is also where wild red salmon thrive, and we enjoy some pretty good (and cheap) meals from these delicious treasures. They are noticeably less fatty than the ones from the farming industry and have a much darker color. We delight in the local empanadas, which we have for snacks, filled with all sorts of local delicacies, meat, seafood, and cheese.

In this part of southern Chile, the Mapuche culture, that of the Indigenous inhabitants of south Chile, is ever-present. One evening, while walking around Frutillar on the shores of Lake Llanquihue, we meet Pedro, a local young man in his twenties. His short size, tanned skin and long, curly, jet-black hair are typical of his ethnicity. Tattoos cover his arms.

He is sitting on the fence of a jetty, playing his bagpipes adorned with a Scottish flag. This is quite an unusual sight. We listen for a while, then strike up a conversation. Pedro left Chile to visit Europe, settled for a time in Scotland, and developed a passion for the instrument. Under the gaze of the Osorno volcano, puffing its regular little smoke rings, Pedro explains the meaning of the tattoos that adorn his arms. One in particular arouses our curiosity: the flag, called the Wenufoye.

It boasts three bands of colors: light blue, green, and red, each bearing the meaning of sacred symbols. In the middle of it is a depiction of the cultrun, the ceremonial Mapuche drum. The circular red design represents the four cardinal points, as well as the stars, the moon, and the sun. The ensemble symbolizes the knowledge of the world, the spirituality and the subtle balance that binds man and all things. My thoughts take me back to Chief Seattle in North America, who was also Indigenous to his lands and who defended nature and the spiritual balance that unites man with his environment.

That evening, without much bitterness but in no uncertain terms, Pedro speaks to us about his country, his culture, and the trees, which have nearly all disappeared since the settlers took possession of the land. Vanishing are the beautiful, tall araucaria (also known as monkey-puzzle) trees that I see everywhere. I call them dinosaur snacks, as both species are dated back to 240 million years ago, the Triassic period! These trees belong here more than we do. How can we even think of getting rid of them?

I often think of Pedro as I continue north and progressively run into more arid lands. During my breaks, I like to sit down and watch the small life that thrives in the forests, taking time to observe a mantis, some butterflies, or, more often, ants. I haven't spent any time observing ants since childhood. But they are quite a show to watch, and I have all the time in the world. As I progress further north, nature becomes more withdrawn and randomly, a series of tree plantations appear by the side of the road, Eucalyptus and pine trees, none of which are native to Chile.

On approaching Los Sauces, I notice two things. One is the increased presence of logging trucks on the country roads, which makes the experience of running on the roads a hair-raising one. The other is the absence of small creatures. I don't see the ants or butterflies anymore. I understand that it is a legacy of the Pinochet Regime and policies of the country. By dispossessing ancestral peoples of their lands and then eradicating native forests to plant rows of eucalyptus and pines, which were more conducive to the timber trade, they in fact erased an entire ecosystem. I move along and hear the Mapuche's cry of distress a little better.

Our first Christmas together on the road turns out to be a bit of a disaster. At the end of a beautiful, sunny run with James by my side, we drive to Villarrica Lake. It's the last of the lakes on our journey and marks a much-awaited rest day. We make the best of our environment, swimming and rowing one of the many colorful wooden canoes for rent. As a treat for the special day, we decide to eat out and dress up for the occasion. We hit the town as the sun goes down, and it soon dawns on us that everything is closed. We had hoped for a nice drink in a café overlooking the lake, then maybe a ceviche or a local fare of salmon. We hop in the van and crisscross the town in search of a shop. The only place open is the petrol station, and the only food they sell are packets of nuts. We sheepishly head back to our place and fix ourselves a dinner of leftovers, with half a packet of spaghetti, a can of chickpeas and two packets of nuts. Not quite the Christmas dinner we had been expecting!

Further north, the lakes and volcanoes give way to vast rivers and dry countryside. I run through a few Reduccions, the Mapuche reservations. Over a million people live in these areas, and though tourists are warned to stay clear of these places, I find nothing but a welcoming culture. I feel safe. The only danger I am wary of is the wildfires. I keep a close eye on it when smoke starts filling the valley. Other than that, we make unhindered progress towards the Pacific coast.

We stop for a few days in Guarilihue, in the heart of the wine region, on the banks of the Itata River. Ivan, a third-generation Mapuche descendant, welcomes us on his land. Ivan is a renowned doctor in anthropology who has embraced his career as an homage to his parents and grandparents. He is also very handy. He has built a beautiful wooden house for guests on the land he co-owns with his partner, Fabio Morales.

He opens his door to us, shows us around his cellars, and tells us about the region's history and the wine-making industry. He takes us for a drive touring his superb vineyards, which do not need irrigation. The soil here drinks in large gulps the ocean's humidity, deposited every morning.

Ivan is very well-versed in the environment and the treasures that abound throughout the country. Just like Pedro in Frutillar, he is attached to the land, to the natural balance of all things, vines, ocean, forests, and fertile soil. What he says makes so much sense. How can we imagine the little impact his voice and his people have today?

We drink Ivan's words and his wines, too! James gets a bit carried away and commits to buying a few boxes of Fabio's wines. The next day, I watch in silence as James loads six crates of wine into the back of the van. How on earth will we get through all this, I wonder? Maybe it is time to swap my traditional post-run beer for a few glasses of local wine. I ponder this thought in my run while crossing a rural part of Chile, which feels very Mediterranean. I am transported by the fragrances in the air: strawberry fields, olive groves, avocado, figs, and vineyards. This is a sensorial reminder of my run around Greece in the summer of 2020.

I reach the Pacific Ocean in Concepción and discover a coastline dotted with quaint fishing villages and low-key resorts. I particularly enjoy the colorful fishing boats, yellow, red, white, and bright blue. One day, James and I watch in awe as one of them returns to shore at full speed to land spectacularly in the middle of the sandy beach. Quite a way to dock! Little shacks, equally colorful, are found nearby, where locals sell their fish, handmade dishes of ceviche, and empanadas.

A beautiful surprise awaits me on the road, the Salinas Lo Valdivia. The historical saltworks are part of only twenty left around the world where salt is collected in the ancient way, a method dating back to the sixteenth century. The road is lined with colored, wooden, open stores selling bags of salt by the kilo. The entire area is United Nations Educational, Scientific and Cultural Organization (UNESCO) classified as a "Living Human Treasure." What a privilege to have discovered this by accident and to witness the workers in their timeless environment, scattered with little dunes of white salt.

As I make my way through the fishing ports along the coast, I see signs indicating evacuation routes in the event of a tsunami. The Chilean coast is particularly exposed, having been devastated many times in the past. Even though I had read about this climatic hazard, I am still shocked to see these signs everywhere, so normalized. I feel the vulnerability of these cities located at sea level, and like them, I am now at the mercy of the ocean's whims.

On the day we arrive in Pichilemu, the weather has a scary twist in store for us. At the end of a scorching hot run, only made bearable by the stunning ocean views, I join James at our stopover for the day. We settle in the wooden cabin we rent for the night by the sea. I then take the van to the neighboring village to find an internet connection to post my blog and GPS data. James stays to stroll along the beach. As I sit at the table in the middle of my work, the alarm on my phone goes off, as does the alarm of all the customers in the café. It's a tsunami alert! I feel a rush of adrenaline.

I hastily gather my belongings with one thing in mind. I need to reach James as fast as I can. Without an Internet connection, alone on this large beach, he is on the front line. Of course, I immediately find myself stuck in traffic jams. Everyone has taken their car and is trying to escape in a mad rush via the only coastal road available.

The four kilometers seem to last forever. James must have left his phone at the cabin, my calls go unanswered. I scan the ocean and panic at the slightest wave that seems to rise on the horizon. I notice the beaches, which were so lively earlier, are deserted now. On the hills facing the sea, I watch people going up in single file, holding hands, to reach the highest points. Tension reaches a new height.

I finally reach the bungalow to find James sitting on the beach, surrounded by a few locals. Chilling out, watching the sun set on the seemingly quiet sea. That British phlegm! He had been alerted by the neighbors, who are on watch and nonchalantly assure us there is nothing to fear. How can they be so sure? Ultimately, the tsunami did not reach the region where we were staying, but it was close. I didn't sleep much that night.

Running along the coast provides me with a great opportunity to observe the wildlife. A different continent means different discoveries, and in Cobquecura, we spend an evening watching sea lions, who live on a small rocky island off the coast. It's the last colony in this part of the world. They are very vocal, and we watch them as the sun sets on the horizon in hues of bright orange and pink. It's like watching a shadow puppet show, the lions cutting black silhouettes against the fiery sky. We stay on the beach until dark, not wanting to miss anything from this spectacle of nature.

Further along, I also get to meet the Inca Terns. They are beautiful black birds with extraordinary white moustaches, yellow cheeks, and red beaks. I spot them mostly near the beaches, taking refuge on stone walls. They make an entertaining sight.

On approach to the capital city of Santiago, I notice the usual sights of increased poverty and harsh living conditions. On the hills of San Antonio, I pass by a few young girls working the streets, dressed unequivocally for the job. The hillsides are scattered with litter and are home to shanty towns made of corrugated metal pieces and wood. But as you go down the hill, you are back into the busy and vibrant streets of the biggest port city in Chile, full of color and activity. I reflect on how the contrasts are always striking when reaching capital cities. They have been this way on all three continents I have crossed so far.

Finally, at the turn of yet another hill along that beautiful coast, I make it to the Pearl of the Pacific, Valparaíso! Built on the hillsides, it is a colorful, lively city covered with murals reminiscent of paintings and splendid works of art steeped in history. Poet Pablo Neruda, a Nobel Prize winner, introduced mural art in 1970s Chile.

After the advent of the Pinochet dictatorship and the ban on all political art, it became vital for the community's survival. The committed artists continued to paint and express themselves under the threat of death and torture. Victor Jara, the popular folk singer and guitar player, had his fingers smashed as he was taunted and tortured, then killed in the central stadium of Santiago, where hundreds of prisoners were being held. The murals, either humorous, peaceful, vindictive, or simply witnesses to history, paint a live fresco which makes the city an artistic treasure. They are a homage to this dark period and an ode to humanity.

We wander Valparaíso's steep streets for a whole day, taking in all the sights. Then, it is finally time to turn our backs on the Pacific Ocean and tackle the colossus that rises to the east, the Andes Mountains. The thought of these mountains gives me shivers. I have been waiting for them, imagining them in so many ways. On the seafront, I try to imagine what the next marathons will be like, up to the top.

20

THE ANDES

Approaching Los Andes, the landscape changes radically at the foot of the Cordillera, and the Chilean Pacific coast is quickly forgotten. Vineyards spread out on the mountainside around me and rise as I move deeper into the Aconcagua Valley. Campesinos on horseback pass, traveling on the dirt roads through all kinds of plantations, primarily fruit. The climb is steady, a few hundred meters each day.

Past Los Andes, the mountains reveal themselves. Around me, no more greenery or cultivated lands. Everything becomes rock, temperatures cool down, and the sun only has a narrow space to make its way between the tall peaks. I am in the heart of the grey cordillera, where nothing grows. I have two demanding days of running in these harsh lands, towards Portillo, at the gates of Argentina.

The ascent to Portillo is impressive. With a positive altitude difference of 1,600 meters, the last part of the run counts thirty-two switchbacks. It is a magnificent, dizzying road where trucks move heavily, in single file like snails weighed down by their cargo. Everything seems to move in slow motion on this tortuous slope. Me included. I had prepared for this day and had come to terms with the idea of alternating between running and walking. Finally, I adopt a slower pace, which allows me to steadily jog all the way. I am very attached to the idea that each portion of this world run is done by running. My GPS data is posted publicly online daily, detailing my progress and statistics, including running speed. Without pressure, I am keen to maintain a pace that leaves no doubt that it is indeed running and not walking.

I pass through seven tunnels on this mountain road, two of which do not have a safety lane. The HGVs pass slowly, allowing me to calculate the moment to launch. I'm dressed in my reflective strips, which make me visible in the dark. Even with these few precautions, it remains a frightening experience.

Halfway there, I meet James on his bike. I notice that his hand is bleeding. He has been pressed against the wall of a tunnel by a truck driver who had not seen him. So close to disaster, it sends shivers down my spine. He is visibly shaken and is heading down below to observe the condors in peace. I make him promise to be more careful. Without his bike lights, he is just as vulnerable as me. I realize how indispensable we have become to each other. I can't wait to finish this climb and find him at the top, safe and sound.

In a state of fatigue, mitigated by a powerful feeling of satisfaction, I reach Portillo, the oldest winter sports resort in Chile. While popular, it is deserted without snow in the mid-season. I head to the refuge for lunch. As I sit in front of the large bay window, I discover before me a contained blue expanse: the Inca Lake. It evokes a little lapis lazuli jewel scintillating in its grey mountain setting. Legend has it that a beautiful princess promised to the Inca prince Yupanqui lost her life on these slopes. She now rests at the bottom of the water, which has taken on the crystalline color of her blue eyes for eternity.

The lake is charming and just as tempting. I ask if it is possible to swim there. The chalet manager smiles at me and replies, "Yes, of course. That's where the Chilean ice-water swimming champion trains!" I laugh heartily. I think I will settle for a hot shower today.

Having reached the high altitude station, we are forced to retrace our steps back to Los Andes for logistical reasons. We need to submit the PCR tests necessary to cross the border. A forty-eight-hour delay, beyond which looms the uncertainty of traveling in times of COVID. I'm never certain that I will be allowed across a border. It puts quite a lot of strain on anyone traveling, let alone two adventurers on a run around the world.

We spend a full afternoon in the yard of the local testing center, amongst dozens of others, mostly truck drivers, waiting for our number to be called under the blazing sun. We get our nose swabbed, then wait again for hours to be given our testing confirmation paper. They "guarantee" to send us our results by email within twenty-four hours.

We spend the next day at the In Situ vineyard, which James had spotted a few days earlier on his bike. We learn more about the region's history and the wine-making tradition. Working conditions are particularly harsh, and the climate and geography make it an unforgiving place. A stark contrast to the gardens of the estate, set amongst a variety of fruit trees: persimmon, olives, oranges, lemons, figs, apples, pears, and quinces. It is a garden of Eden from which to watch and supervise work on the tortuous slopes.

We drive back up to Portillo at 2,870m and at dawn, I run to the border post, where James is waiting for me in the minivan. The logistics are hectic. I make sure all the papers are in order. We are not confident. I received my results this morning, but James' are still marked as "pending." I need to be with him at the border post. If anything goes wrong, we'll have to stay put in Los Andes and go through the process one more time.

Just as I present all our paperwork to the officer on duty, he brushes my PCR test result to the side. All we need is the vaccination certificate! Rules and requirements are changing daily, and it appears that we could have forgone these two days of waiting in Los Andes. At least the situation is favorable to us, and we are free to head towards Argentina without the PCR test result.

Ahead of us, the road is closed to pedestrians and cyclists for the next twenty kilometers. It's a bit of a no man's land. We have stamped our way out of Chile, but we will not cross the Argentinian border post until tomorrow, and I will have to reach it by trail. I begin the ascent on the mountainside. James parks the minivan on the side of the road and gets on his bike. The path that leads to the summit winds over fifty-two switchbacks. At each turn, I plunge a little deeper into the heart of the Andes through increasingly arid, isolated, and immense settings of splendid grey hues. I climb to almost 4,000 meters above sea level. What exhilaration! The effort is noticeably more marked, but I can't tell if it's due to the lack of oxygen or the stifling altitude difference. Certainly, both.

James pedals, films, and takes photos. It's difficult for him too. While I usually enjoy my solitude during my run, I feel infinite gratitude towards him for being here today to share this wonderful moment with me. How can I explain the feeling that takes over my entire being as I move forward? Without the world run, I would never be standing here. Few people take this path, even fewer by running or cycling. Everything that is offered to me, these landscapes, these sensations of heightened freedom, these discoveries at each bend, I owe only to this magnificent journey that I had dared to dream.

At the last bend, I spot the imposing statue of Cristo Redentor (Christ the Redeemer), standing on a dazzling white promontory. The Chilean and Argentinian flags planted on either side symbolize the demarcation between the two countries. It was built in 1904 to signify the end of a conflict between the neighbors. This bronze giant gives me the most beautiful border crossing of the entire adventure. The highest point, conquered at the cost of a colossal effort.

I'm euphoric. What a feeling to be here with my head above the clouds and a smile on my lips. Standing under the stunning blue sky, scanning the horizon and the surrounding peaks. Among them is the giant of the Andes, the Aconcagua, which rises to almost 7,000 meters. It's the highest peak in the world outside the Himalayan range. I also think about Tom Denniss, who almost lost his life on these slopes as he crossed the Andes in snow and ice conditions in November 2012.

But everything is perfect today, and I'm in a festive mood. It gets chilly fast at this altitude, and I'm starting to get the shivers. Surprisingly, in this unlikely place, there is a small hut of souvenirs and chocolate specialties from Argentina. I wonder why on earth anyone would set a stall here. Then, I understand that on the eastern side, the dirt road is accessible to vehicles.

A man guards the entrance. He spots me and brings two glasses of strong alcohol. I run my nose over the one he hands me, and the strong vapors clear my sinuses instantly. He raises his glass with me, and we drink down. He laughs when he sees me bent in half, hands on my thighs, struggling to breathe. It has its effect!

James joins me and we go inside to take shelter from the wind. The owner comes back with three glasses and some chunks of delicious local chocolate. It must be rare for foreigners to arrive here by running and cycling. I have another swig, and presto, I feel the temperature rising!

We stay in silence for a long while in the warmth of this makeshift cabin, a little stunned to be here. The place is so surreal. The effect of the spirit eventually wears off, and the cold hits me again. I will have to think about starting my way downhill, around the bends, which will lead me to another valley on the Argentinian side. James must go back to the minivan and drive through the tunnels to find me further down the road. We no longer have a means of communication. Our Chilean SIM cards do not work here, and it will be at least two days until we can purchase Argentinian ones. We rely on each other to be careful. The fright we got in the tunnels yesterday is still fresh in our minds.

I put on my windbreaker and set off again. I thought the descent was going to be easy, but it isn't. I curse my excitement at the summit, which made me down those two glasses of liquor. My head is heavy. I feel nauseous. What a stupid idea to have done this halfway through the run, at an altitude of 4000m, when I still have around twenty kilometers to go. I fume while trying to concentrate on running down the switchbacks. I have never had so much difficulty going down, and I see the ribbon of asphalt down below, which taunts me, always seeming so far away at the turn of each bend.

When I finally get to the road, I am exhausted. My head feels like it weighs a ton, but I decide to continue. I hope that James gets to my level as quickly as possible so I can stop my run before the planned forty kilometers. The valley is magnificent, and I wind through its heart, surrounded by dark and imposing mountains, which only reveal a thin streak of blue sky. On my left, a wooden gate marks the start of the path leading hikers to the Aconcagua summit. I envy the few adventurers I see preparing their equipment. The conditions are ideal. Before long, they will be treading on the giant of the Andes. I have tasted a bit of the exhilaration of the summits in the past, climbing up to 6,200 meters in the Himalayas, but I have not yet stepped on the tallest roofs in the world. Maybe someday …

These light thoughts help me forget my migraine, but I now have another problem to deal with: heavy truck traffic, which is hair-raising. Uphill on the Chilean slopes, their lumbering made them harmless, but on the Argentinian side, at full speed in the descent?

The trucks' wheels are equipped with an additional braking system, a sort of mechanical chrome arm which gives them a strange futuristic appearance. Despite this safety measure, I feel very vulnerable on my narrow roadside, protected from these behemoths with articulated wheels by a simple line of white paint.

The next day, I run while James drives the van to the border post, where we meet to mark our entry to Argentina. Again, we cross our fingers that we will be allowed into the country. We have our insurance papers, vaccination certificates, PLF forms, online questionnaire, vehicle stamps and authorization to cross. After a long and stressful wait, we are finally clear to continue our way. I trot through the border post by the side of the van and breathe a massive sigh of relief.

Around me, the mountains seem to come to life. The shades of ochre, red, green, and purple, and all the deposits of sediments accumulated over millennia give color and life back to this otherwise grey cordillera. Along Ruta 7, I discover the remains of the Camino del Inca, the path taken by the pre-Columbians around 1480 BC. There is an old bridge with remains of dwellings, and I am amazed that the site is not protected. It is left as is with a simple sign and a few lines to describe the progress of archaeological research. Yet another open-air treasure.

After two days of running down the valley, I see an oasis on the horizon. On both sides of the banks of the Rio Uspallata, there is vegetation and greenery at last. It's the first Argentinian city of my crossing. 1,400 kilometers now separate me from Buenos Aires on the Atlantic coast. Arriba!

21

¡ARRIBA BUENOS AIRES!

Under the long shadow cast by the domineering Aconcagua, I head towards Mendoza, another world-famous wine region. With a new country comes new culinary delights. Running-wise, the road to Buenos Aires is flat. I should not cross any significant mountains or hills, and it is set to be hot. Scorching hot.

I will have company for a week. A French journalist, Franck, had contacted me a while back to write an article about my journey. He thought he would get a better understanding if he were running by my side. Seven marathons in a row are quite a heavy price to pay to get a better view of the world run. And though I don't know him at all, I let him join the expedition. I figure if he is too tired at any point, he has the option of getting in the van with James.

I wonder if this one week will allow Franck to feel all of what I experienced on the road. The specificity and beauty of this adventure represents the culmination of my desires and dreams. I am aware that if, from my point of view, the effort of the daily marathon is anecdotal, for a passenger who joins the adventure over a short period, this will surely represent the essence of the experience. I hope he, too, will be able to experience the world differently, feel its grandeur and understand the value of traveling on foot.

We meet with him in Mendoza on my rest day. James drives me around the city center, and I spend the afternoon getting to know Franck. Then, it's time for James and me to retreat to our hotel. We walk out towards the van. Except, we cannot remember where we parked it. All the streets look alike, and there are outdoor car parks scattered throughout the city. We crisscross the city for over two hours before we eventually locate it.

We make it just in time before the car park closes and are asked to pay in cash. That's how we discover the magic blue exchange rate. If you change your American dollars in the street, you get twice as many pesos as you would in a bank. The Argentinian economy is in such a dire state that people would do anything to get their hands on the steady dollar. This will surely make crossing this country by far the cheapest of the journey.

The Argentine Pampas spread as far as the eye can see, and summer is now in full swing. There are no trees to provide shade and no mountains or hills to hide from the sun. It is going to hit hard! On the menu for Franck, there are 287 kilometers of running with me to San Luis, seven stages of forty-one kilometers, completely flat and under the direct sun, in temperatures that soar way beyond forty degrees Celsius. We set off on a small country road along the vineyard fields. There is no mistake. It is indeed the Argentinian wine capital that we are traveling through. At each break, I look back at the snow-capped peak of Aconcagua, seemingly melting in the distance.

During this week of running together, we move from the Andes to the plains, then from secondary roads to Ruta 7, the main road leading to Buenos Aires. We pass through a series of rural villages from one province to another, sleep in makeshift cabins of questionable hygiene, and enjoy the cool air of the evening around the barbecue prepared by James. Under the stars, we drink wine and listen to music. What can Franck think of this nomadic lifestyle that is so familiar to me? He seems most concerned about the pain in his legs and the harsh climate, which is taking away all his energy. Every day, he suffers through most of the run and then shares with me all his ailments.

I question myself again about the mystery of my physiological adaptation. So far, I have had no injuries, no cramps, I have not had heavy legs, and I have not been sick. I did not follow a particular diet. It varied considerably depending on the regions crossed: from the burgers and frozen pizzas of North America to the Mediterranean diet rich in proteins and lipids of southern Europe. I did not take any dietary supplements, anti-inflammatories, gels, or energy drinks. I have not precisely calculated the number of calories consumed each day, but I estimate that it rarely went beyond 3,000 kcal. I didn't use massages or stretching. My water consumption during the daily marathon varied from 200 ml in the middle of winter to six liters during the heatwave of summer 2020.

The French National Institute of Sport, Exercise and Performance looked briefly at my case, in order to analyze my body's adaptation mechanisms. Unfortunately, I had already been engaged in my adventure for over a year when I caught their attention. Without the comparison of before and after or an upstream development of data collection and analysis protocols, they decided they couldn't start a study on my physiological adaptations. It was a disappointment. I would have liked to understand the mechanisms of my body, and study what could have strengthened my immune system to this extent while protecting my muscles, joints, and bones.

The town of San Martin offers me a very amusing and unexpected meeting. As we stroll through the streets in search of a place to eat, I stumble upon a three-meter-tall statue of Mafalda in the main square. What a thrill! I had no idea that Quino, the cartoonist, was from here. I climb up by Mafalda's side to pose for a photo with this little mischievous girl who is as stubborn as I am, and incidentally boasts the same haircut I do. It's an incredible coincidence to meet her here. If she had not emerged from the tip of my pen in 2017, during an interminable telephone conversation at the office, would I be here? Would I be standing in front of her, en route to making my life's dream come true?

When Franck leaves, I find myself alone on the road again. For his part, James is busy uncovering the secrets and treasures of the railway line, whose route we are now following. He came upon its beginnings in the Andes and discovered that the engineering was essentially British from the last century—an impromptu occasion to reconnect with his country's history.

The track is now abandoned, but each village we pass through proudly preserves these locomotives as vestiges of a not-so-distant past. The similarity with North America is striking. There is a railway line, plantations on both sides and grain silos with a few homes every fifty kilometers. The unmistakable mark of the pioneers.

Following their trail, James leads me through the countryside on the dirt roads that run alongside the abandoned rails. He scouts ahead on his bike and guides me with directions far from road traffic into the heart of nature. Off the beaten track, the sounds of trucks and cars are pleasantly replaced by birds and parrots, often flying by my side in a raucous jumble of cackles and tweets.

On the sand, I spot the imprints of snakes and other reptiles. I watch for them, and sometimes, I am rewarded. I cross paths with the magnificent black and white tegus, a type of large lizard endemic to South America, as well as the local dwarf armadillos. These trails are not on the maps. Even Google Maps does not have them. Thanks to his cycling recces, James offers me a unique adventure. Alone, I would undoubtedly have followed the busy and noisy Ruta 7 all the way.

The Córdoba and Santa Fe provinces bring about changes in the environment and running conditions. The agricultural fields give way to marshes. The region is very humid, on par with tropical areas, and the roadsides are often flooded. This means one important thing to me. Mosquitos are everywhere. They try and fly into my nose and mouth while I run, never leaving me in peace for long. During my breaks, they make a meal out of me, prompting me to resume running earlier than I would have wanted.

Yet, in the small villages, we find people who give us the best welcome. Just like in North America, it is in the most isolated places that I (and now we) stand out most. The region we are crossing is not touristy at all. Runners and cyclists are a rare sight. We receive many acts of kindness. I get a haircut for free at a salon where Roberta, the owner, is happy to just practice her French in exchange. One night, we share our barbecue dinner with neighbors and are gifted a bottle of wine. When we tend to a dog who has been hit by a car, strangers come to our rescue to help get him to the vet. In San Gregorio, the whole staff of the restaurant poses with us for a picture and entertains us all evening. The next day, they get up at dawn to wave us off at the departure of my run. We enjoy greatly the simplicity and welcoming ways of these places, seldom featuring a place to enjoy a coffee or a meal.

On the way to Chacabuco, we encounter heavy rain that suddenly turns all the nice trails into a muddy affair. Twelve kilometers into the run, I spot the van in the distance ... in a ditch! The tires of the Condor Camper are rather slick, and James lost control as it slipped sideways across the path. James, with his usual calm demeanor, does not seem to be too worried about it. A local has passed him in a Jeep and promised to come back. And he does. Minutes later, two men arrive driving sturdy pickup trucks, and though James doesn't speak a word of Spanish, he directs the operations and before long, the van is back on the muddy trail.

We offered money to our kind rescuers, who would not accept it. In the end, James gave them our last two bottles of Chilean wine, all that remained of our six cases purchased from Ivan in Guarilihue.

As we get closer to Buenos Aires, the trails disappear, and Ruta 7 becomes my only option. There is more traffic, and I have to run on the grassy verge, which is mostly inconvenient. I cannot see what I step on, and I recall a few scary brushes, notably with some hidden potholes and snakes.

I set off on the last segment of the road towards Buenos Aires and the coincidence of the calendar has one more surprise in store for me. Since I'm supposed to reach the Argentine capital on March 8, International Women's Rights Day, I reconnect with the consular network. They have always accompanied and supported me, announcing the date of my arrival, and welcoming me warmly. The consulate transfers me to the embassy, which I am told will be better suited to give me a suitable welcome.

I soon understand why. It is not an ambassador I am to meet but an Ambassadress, Claudia Scherer-Effosse. A polyglot diplomat with a brilliant international career, she travels the world with panache. I am told she is preparing celebrations for March 8 in this country, which has only recently opened up to the issues of equality and diversity. She is planning a reception on the theme of women in sport for the occasion. It couldn't have come at a better time!

On March 8, 2022, I cross the last circle of the Buenos Aires suburbs, which leads to the heart of the megacity on the Atlantic coast. James is driving the minivan alone, on the eight-lane highway that leads to the capital. He has no GPS, as his phone data expired the previous night, and I wonder how he will ever find me in this city of ten million people! The only direction I have given him is that the French school is located by the ocean. I wrote down the name of the park next to it. It is a miracle that he manages to find me there at all.

I turn into the street of the French school and spot a crowd in the distance. A woman in sportswear comes forward to welcome me, Laurence Leyendecker, the director of the establishment. The students by the dozen follow suit, and soon, there are more than a hundred of us running through the park adjacent to the high school. Then, another silhouette stands out in the distance. Shorts and a black T-shirt, a huge smile across her face, I know it's her. Madam Ambassador! She is not wearing an evening dress nor offering me to dig into a pyramid of hazelnut chocolates. She dons her sports shoes to give her presence to mark the symbolically important day and event.

We end up in the school's courtyard, where hundreds of students form a guard of honor, applauding as we pass. This moment is so unusual when you have just crossed an entire continent alone, with few accolades. Although James provides support on the journey, the fact remains that my daily marathon is still a solo effort.

To celebrate this special day, I spend the afternoon in the Lycée's amphitheater, talking with the students. The classes parade past me, one after the other. I present to them the world run. The dialogue begins and they question me about the commitment I have chosen for the benefit of a women's NGO. I reflect on how I am part of a French generation who has benefited from the tremendous advances made towards rights and autonomy by the women of my mother's and grandmother's generation. My commitment reflects that the acquisition of rights and emancipation is far from universal. Argentina is a good example, having only legalized abortion the year before.

I realize these young people are much more educated on gender issues than I was at their age. I learned through our discussions that Argentina, which has just begun debating parity, already includes this subject in the students' curriculum. Working men must also attend seminars on gender equality. A tremendous leap forward. The children's interventions are relevant, precise, and full of optimism. I will not have much time to rest. As soon as the question-and-answer game is over, I barely have enough time to attend the Ambassadress' reception.

The third continental crossing ends on a festive note, in the brightly colored streets of El Caminito, the cradle of the tango in Buenos Aires. We raise a glass to the sound of the accordions and celebrate with James these three months of crossing. I notice that the further the journey progresses, the more it gives in return. James seems to have succumbed to the charm of my extreme nomadic existence. His decision has been made. He will accompany me across Australia, too.

22

THE BODY

In over two years of running, I have not had a single injury or even been sick. Better, over time, I have managed to increase my distances. Running six days a week, my average is still above forty kilometers per day. I have pushed the cursor regularly beyond fifty kilometers throughout the US crossing. In August 2021, I ran my longest stage, sixty-four kilometers from Terry to Glendive, Montana, and it went just fine. I test myself and experiment cautiously. The journey involves running long distances every day over several years. Whatever I do needs to be done with the view of preserving my health rather than seeking performance at all costs.

Endurance is not just about physical capacity. I know many who are more muscular, leaner, trained, and better coached than me. However, I know few people who would run a four-and-a-half-hour marathon a day for more than two years, six days a week, without getting injured, whilst having tremendous fun doing it. The expression "It's all in the mind" is often overused, but there is a lot of truth to it. What you run for, the feedback you get, and the reward you seek from it are closely correlated to the pleasure you derive from it.

Throughout my preparation, I did not want to let numbers dictate my feedback and feelings. In my view, a "good" run had to be appreciated by factors other than metric indicators such as speed, pace, or cardiac rhythm. I learned to run by feeling only and connect with my environment while doing it. It occurred to me that I had many constraints at work and that numbers and time dictated a major part of how I lived my life. Running free of stress and in nature provided me with a perfect occasion to disconnect from numbers and reconnect with the world and myself.

The state of mind with which I approach a run will often influence its outcome. Any performance pressure I had put on myself in the past, in training and racing, had affected my feelings about the run. It is a natural tendency to want to better oneself and win against others. Competition leads to pushing oneself past the point where the body starts sending signals that it is uncomfortable. We are taught to push past to improve.

It appeared important to define precisely what I was seeking out of the journey and formulate it simply in the same way companies establish their mission statement. Something that will always be at the forefront of my mind, my true north. "I run around the world, to gather a unique experience of it through my five senses, let it surprise me, and enjoy it to the fullest." I coined that simple statement at the beginning of my preparation, and it did not change throughout the entire journey. That was all I needed to know to get up every morning with an appetite for the run and the day ahead.

When I get ready each morning, I review the planned route on Google Maps. I envision myself on these roads and trails. I imagine where I could take my breaks, the places that are suitable for it. I think of the new destination that awaits me and the surprises my journey has in store. Then, I mentally divide the distance into affordable segments and find something I'm looking forward to in each of them. I never fail to be surprised. That's why I have good runs every day, no matter the weather or terrain conditions.

I trust my body because I have trained it specifically for this adventure. But I also watch it closely. Running magazines and specialized websites are full of programs for completing a marathon in a target time and preparing for your first half or ultramarathon. But there is no guide for runners who want to do seven hundred marathons in a row. It doesn't exist, or at least no one has written it yet. I had a statistic clearly in mind: between 50 and 70 percent of runners (the range is wide, depending on the sources) aiming for a marathon get injured during their preparation. If there is one thing I must avoid, it is precisely injury.

In this adventure, my body is my main ally and means of transport. Without it, the journey stops, and the dream becomes just a dream again. With this in mind, it seemed unthinkable to me to delegate the management of this extremely important tool to anyone else. I had to be my own expert and learn all I could about how my body works. The same went for training. I didn't seek advice from a coach because I felt that the project called for a completely different approach from what was traditionally accepted and required an unconventional mindset. Since it was my brainchild, I led the project and fully assumed the responsibilities that arose from it. I would train, learn physiology, and understand biomechanics. I would gradually define, by trial and error, the volume of training which will prepare me in the best conditions for the daily marathon, which will be my norm.

Such an atypical project called for atypical solutions. In terms of training, I no longer worried about time and running pace. Only mileage mattered on routes where I calculated the distance in advance. No watch on my wrist and, above all, no speed exercises. Since I was preparing to run slowly and sustainably, this is exactly what I needed to practice, and nothing else. This had the advantage of significantly reducing my risk of injury. I also made mastering biomechanics my main objective.

I chose a physiotherapist to help me with this task, and again, in an unconventional way. My choice narrowed down to Padraig, a thirty-something Irishman based in Singapore who specialized in football and rugby. It seemed wise for me to avoid a running specialist, who would necessarily know that it is impossible to run marathons day after day without recovery, massages, or injury. Padraig offered me a fresh perspective devoid of preconceptions. I trusted his professionalism and his desire to support me in my preparation. The mission I assigned to him was simple. I visited him every month, and he observed me on the treadmill and in the execution of stability exercises. If he noticed any change or degradation in my posture or movements, he'd teach me how to identify the problem, and we'd work together on solutions.

I learned proprioception with him. I analyzed and corrected my posture primarily by feeling, with some visual aid. His observations, as well as the mirror that hung near the treadmill, helped me refine my perception. To cope with the increased volume of work that one puts it through, the body has a natural tendency to spare itself as much as possible. This often results in an additional load on the joints to protect a muscle that disengages. A guaranteed recipe for injury. Padraig taught me to run by feeling and to call for the action of specific muscles.

I also took advantage of his experience to correct my stride. My landing now occurs on the ball of the foot to optimize cushioning and spare my joints. The anatomy charts are clear. The foot is made of twenty-six bones, thirty-three joints, and more than one hundred muscles, tendons, and ligaments. These are designed for the essential roles of cushioning, stabilizing, and propelling. No running shoe with a propylene heel, air cushions, or carbon sole will come close to the formidable intelligence and natural construction of the foot!

This also explains why I am impervious to running shoe brands and gimmicks. My only criteria are the thickness of the sole (minimal) and the drop between the heel and the toes (also minimal). I understand that if I let my foot do the job it is designed to do, I should be able to optimize my mechanics, naturally strengthen it, and avoid injuries.

During my two years of preparation, whether my daily twenty-kilometer commute or marathons-journey trips, I established a routine: the body scan. No run escaped its rigor, and I spent as much time as was required on it. An hour or ten minutes, it didn't matter, as long as it was thorough. I start with my toes. I feel them mentally. I try to identify if there are tensions, pressure points, or friction. Then I move up. The sole, along its length, then the top of it, the ankles, and then the entire body up to the base of the neck. I don't let anything slip, showing total intransigence. At the slightest signal, I concentrate and analyze. It could be something benign, shoelaces that are too tight or chafing sock seams. But it can also be problems related to posture, alignment, degraded movements, or external factors such as terrain and weather conditions. I listen to everything. I attend to minor signals to prevent major injuries. And it works.

I sometimes submit to the scan several times a day. I linger and acquire a taste for it. This is also why I run without music, so I don't distract myself from my environment and my sensations. It is a constant task to keep the machine in good working order when the daily load is so heavy. I have no appetite for pain and do not subscribe to the motto, "no pain, no gain," which often prevails in the running world. I prefer to move forward calmly, in good health and intelligence, putting in all the effort and energy that it requires. Better ten minutes of calm concentration on the tension point than bursts of speed causing injuries.

The irony is that the only injury I have suffered thus far is to my fingers! Arms and hands are the only body parts not included in my daily body scan. Would this injury have occurred if I had subjected my fingers to the same analytical rigor as the rest of my body?

I ran while pushing a thirty-kilo stroller for two years across Europe and North America. This gave me an atypical musculature for a marathon runner, like broad shoulders and back, powerful thighs and glutes. Every day, throughout my daily marathons, my hands gripped and opened rhythmically to catch and propel Bob in rhythm with my strides. These unusual and repeated movements, applied to a significant load, wore out my hands. My index, ring, and middle fingers suffered from trigger finger syndrome one after the other. The flexor tendon inflamed, swelled, and became blocked in its sheath, leaving the fingers stuck in a bent position. It can be quite painful. The answer to this problem was simple. I increased the diameter of my handlebar so that my fingers no longer had to bend and grab it. Etienne, a journalist I met and who welcomed me in his town of Vesoul in February 2021, helped me in this task. He drove me to the local DIY store, and we bought heating insulation tubes. We wrapped them around the handlebar, and magic happened. I was able to push with the flat of my hand, and the wounds eventually healed on their own.

I learned my lesson, and it has reinforced the importance of the daily body scan. Listen to your body. Get to know it well. Study the anatomy charts. Refine your feelings. Practice proprioception to open a dialogue. I think it would be a mistake, in this type of project, to rely solely on specialists. We gain much more by seeking to understand ourselves by taking an in-depth interest in the mechanisms of the human body rather than promptly referring to an expert who will always lack the finesse of perception with the problems we feel.

The human body is made for running. It is its most natural activity. The anatomy of the foot, tendons and ligaments, the way our neck moves independently from our head, the rotation of the shoulders, the skeleton, and our muscles have evolved to make man an endurance runner, capable of hunting to the point of exhaustion for his survival. The concept has been well documented in numerous studies as well as in Christopher McDougall's book, *Born to Run*. Even if I'm not running for my survival, I feel something deeply organic and ancestral when my body moves through the world in harmony, in the most natural way possible.

23

LAST CONTINENT, AUSTRALIA

This continent has been a long time coming! In my initial projection, Oceania should have directly succeeded Europe in the order of the world run. Instead, it comes last. Its doors had remained closed for a long time after the health crisis, and it is only since March 2022 that foreigners have been welcome again. Upon returning from Buenos Aires, we submit our visa applications, and after five long weeks of waiting, we fly to the Antipodes.

We make a remarkable entry into Australian territory. On the plane that takes us on the West Coast to Perth, we fill out a bunch of arrival forms and all kinds of declarations, including a bio-hazard questionnaire. Local authorities are notoriously strict on this subject. Bringing any non-native bacteria in your luggage is a no-no. You cannot pack as much as an apple from your homeland. We disembark and collect our luggage, as well as James' bike and my stroller, from the carousel. Then we go through the various checks. A man in uniform signals to us. We are going to be searched.

As the agent approaches to open the front pocket of James' suitcase, my adrenaline level goes through the roof. Oh no! The three months of running across South America immediately come to my mind. James has a weakness for spring onions. One day, as he bit into a raw onion at the finish of my run, I told him how much I despised the smell that sticks to the breath and skin. He was amused by such strong feelings towards a completely innocuous vegetable and began a little game that lasted until Buenos Aires.

From that moment on, I regularly found a spring onion in my socks, bag, or stuffed into my running shoes. I never mentioned anything, but each time I discovered one, I'd hide it back in James' belongings. At the bottom of his toiletry bag, with his toothbrush, or in this case, one of the multiple pockets of his suitcase. The onion traveled from his bag to mine without us ever discussing it—a silly prank. But during the five weeks of transit, we have forgotten all about its whereabouts. It has remained in its last hiding place, which James had not yet discovered.

In good faith, I try to explain this little joke to the officer, who does not find the story as amusing as we do. She proceeds to open said pocket, extracts the guilty onion, and places it in an airtight bag, which she seals before our eyes. The dreaded evidence bag.

This is how we find ourselves accused of attempting to import a cultivable product. With his legendary calm, James explains to the agent that, given the state of the vegetable, it would be difficult to try to cultivate it. The argument falls flat.

The rest of our luggage goes under the microscope. James is ordered to take his bike out of its protective cover. Upon careful inspection, dried mud marks are discovered on the side of the tires. Indefensible. We head to the cleaning station, where we are ordered to clean the wheels. We wash and scrape the rims to perfection, cautious that we must show our goodwill in the matter so as not to infuriate anyone.

The customs lady chief orders me to open my bag and asks if I have some tent pegs. The mixture of stress and fatigue hits me badly, and I cannot make out what she is saying, I understand “toothpaste” instead of “tent pegs”. I can see that this misunderstanding irritates her further. She proceeds to inspect the contents of my bag with forensic precision and finds a few grains of sand under the soles of my running shoes. She holds them up to me like a trophy. Back to the cleaning station we go, to make sure the soles are free of any foreign body.

We are both upset and tired. It has been a long journey, but we try to keep as calm as possible. The lady in charge finally comes back, handing us our bills. I am charged $2,600 for the onion. James gets a bill of $400 for the bicycle wheels. Is it out of benevolence or negligence that she turns a blind eye to my running shoes? The pill is hard to swallow, and there is no immediate recourse available to us. The budget of the world run is seriously dented.

I am boiling inside, but I know I cannot express any anger. It would only make matters worse. James settles his fine on the spot while I decide to sleep on mine. On the way to our hotel, I realize that they have charged me for an onion that was found inside James’ bag. A clear procedural flaw which gives me a legitimate ground for appeal. I withhold the story from my daily blog, fearing the appeal committee does any research on my journey and finds derogatory comments. After two weeks of waiting, my fine is reduced to $1,300, though not cancelled. Still, a damn hefty price to pay for a dried-up spring onion.

Our first day in the country has a bitter taste. We are in a hurry to move forward and put this matter at bay. As if to cure me of my anger, the first few days of running are magical. Cottesloe Beach has been the starting place of many of my marathon journeys. I have stood here many times before, my back to the Indian Ocean for the beginning of an adventure. I run on trails I have explored before, towards Middle Swan and Lake Leschenaultia. I have vivid and pleasant memories of running and setting up camp in these places, intensified by the excitement of these first training tests.

I reconnect with the emotions of what my exotic discoveries were back then: the green and yellow budgies, a type of parrot you see everywhere in the Perth region, the Galah, a pink and grey cockatoo that make a racket when they fly together in large flocks. I recall the kookaburra, too, that small bird with a wide and large beak whose joyous song is so uplifting. I am less looking forward to the magpies, which can notoriously be quite aggressive, but fortunately, we are outside the nesting season. We should not be the target of their terrifying dives. Snakes are hibernating this season, which is one worry out of the way. But the flies are causing me problems, forcing me to run with a net over my head. I tread on the red sand of the trails, amongst the fragrant silver-green eucalyptus trees and shrublands so typical of this faraway land, transported by a flow of strong emotions.

We inaugurate a new means of transport on this crossing. It is now at the wheel of a motorhome that James takes care of the logistics, driving every morning to the arrival point before getting on his bike. Our house on wheels should allow us total autonomy, which will be useful in the vastly unpopulated lands that open before us.

Equipped with a shower, a small gas stove and toilets, we will be able to move forward self-sufficiently wherever the day's stage takes us. At this point of the journey, James has committed to accompanying me through the Nullarbor Plains and plans to head back to Europe afterwards. It means that I have my stroller with me and am preparing to finish the world run alone in Sydney.

Past Perth, the Swan and Avon Rivers provide a beautiful backdrop to our adventure amongst the greenery of suburbia before the landscapes start turning arid. We quickly find ourselves following in the footsteps of the early gold prospectors, roaming from village to village or between settlements. Unlike North and South America, it is not the course of the railway lines that I follow but the pipeline. Water is scarce here, there are no lakes or rivers. I follow its course for 600 kilometers on red sand trails, close to the main road but isolated and surrounded by nature. The enormous pipeline runs straight to the largest gold mine in the world, Kalgoorlie.

I meet the cyclists of the Pipeline Challenge one morning, riding in teams, accompanied by their support vehicles. They are on a fabulous five-day adventure "from the red dirt of the Goldfields to the green of the Perth hills." A group of them stop by as I sit down for a break. We exchange stories and share snacks. These cyclists seem to live on a diet of gummy bears! They leave me with a full bag of the delicacies and a donation for Woman for Woman International before pedaling away in a cloud of red dust.

Southern Cross is renowned for being the site of the first major gold discovery in 1887. The water pipeline, which runs from Mundaring to Kalgoorlie, was the backbone of the gold digger's settlements on what is now known as the Golden Pipeline Heritage Trail, where I am running.

At the local museum, James strikes up a conversation with an Aboriginal woman working there, who proceeds to give us a piece of the history of her people through her personal story. It is eerily similar to the one recounted in the movie "Rabbit-Proof Fence," which was filmed just outside the town.

She grew up in a time, not so long ago, when settlers removed Aboriginal children from their families, a practice which lasted until 1969. She belongs to this "stolen generation," and we are overcome with sadness as she recounts the poignant moment when she was taken away from her siblings. She hears the last words of her mother, "Never forget who your father was."

It was the last time she saw or heard from her parents. The treatment formerly reserved for native communities constitutes an unhealed wound across the country, and the anecdote takes me back to the memory of the Mapuche of Chile and the Native Americans from North America.

Before reaching Kalgoorlie, the most emblematic city of the Australian gold rush, we set up camp in nature for the first time. From where I finish my run, we drive to a side road taking us off the Great Eastern Highway and park the motorhome fifty meters deep. In the forested area, amongst the fragrances of eucalyptus trees, we find a cool area to escape the afternoon sun.

I use the van's shower facility for the first time, nothing too luxurious, but it does the job. Then we collect wood for our barbecue and end up face-to-face with a group of emus. The flightless birds run for their lives, clearly not thrilled to see us on their turf. In the evening, though, we spot a few curious ones circling our home a few times before vanishing silently into the night. I guess we are the strange creatures over here!

The area seems to abound with gold seekers. Widgiemooltha welcomes the traveler with a gold-painted replica of the biggest nugget uncovered on location. It also features a roadhouse, the first on our journey. I was curious about what they looked like, having heard so much about them but never seeing one before. They are, in fact, nothing more than a little motel with a bar attached to it, serving drinks and basic food. Very low-key and simple. There's also an area outside where we can plug in the motorhome and use the communal toilet and shower facilities. They close very early at night, and by nine p.m., everything is silent. A perfect setting to take it all in and watch a new sunset over a new landscape. Sitting outside, we meet our neighbor, a gold digger in his forties, who happens to be preparing his stock market report, sitting in a camping chair, and dressed as a construction worker with mud on his boots!

I start seeing signs that I am getting closer to the long and dreaded desert crossing. One morning, I come across a road train assembly area. This is quite an impressive sight. The long trucks that cross the country from side to side, connecting the West and East Coast, look just like normal HGVs, except they pull two or three wagons and measure up to fifty meters. They are proper mastodons of the road and generate a massive blow when passing a tiny runner on the side of the road at high speed. Danger ahead!

From there, we head south towards Norseman, which will mark the beginning of the Nullarbor Plain, a semi-desert devoid of water and people. But before we get there, James experiences another setback. He inadvertently reverses the motorhome over his bike, and one of his wheels is a complete write-off. Quite a stroke of bad luck, and we are kilometers away from any big city. We have no choice but to take a long drive back. What will he do through the plains without a bike? On my next rest day, we drive 200 kilometers back to Kalgoorlie. The only bike shop we find does not have a wheel fit for James' bike. Catastrophe. Seeing how distraught we are, the owner offers to sell us his own very expensive carbon wheels. The bike is fixed, but that was another costly mistake!

24

NULLARBOR WILDERNESS

Past Norseman, things look very different. Before us, the Nullarbor stretches over 1,200 kilometers of semi-desert plains. On the program is a single road, the Eyre Highway, dotted with roadhouses every 100 or 200 kilometers on average. These oases are places of passage for all the truckers who cross the country in their road trains, but also for the rare tourists or cyclists who set out on an adventure. There is not a single village, grocery store, or anything else on this long road from Norseman to Ceduna.

On our first day in the Nullarbor, we realize that our propane gas can is empty. We probably won't be able to find a replacement throughout the crossing. All we have for cooking is our barbecue. As for showers, it will be cold water from now on. As we hit the Balladonia Roadhouse, more bad news hits. We won't be able to replenish our water reserve along the way due to a shortage. The curse of the Australia trip continues! So much for being self-sufficient. But we adapt as always, and things are not as bad as they seem.

Stopping in the middle of nowhere amid wild and magnificent settings, looking for a campsite among the eucalyptus trees, preparing the barbecue, and washing outdoors in a small basin because the water reserve is running low. We read or play cards in the evenings when we are out of internet range. We appreciate these moments away from everything, disconnected from civilization, time, and social norms. We observe wild nature and take time to listen to the birds. I spot a few fairy wrens, tiny birds with bright blue tails, and we feed some magpies, too, which I discover are very social, curious creatures. When we are lucky, we are rewarded by the soaring flight of the wedge-tailed eagle silhouetted against the piercing blue sky.

The Eyre Highway cuts straight through the habitat of many species. In these landscapes of shrubland and mallee woodland, kangaroos thrive. During my marathons, I sometimes spot them bouncing in the distance, but far too often, I see their bones along the road as well, a nearly continuous stream. They are not protected from the highway in any way.

One morning, while I am running in the early hours towards the Cocklebiddy Roadhouse, I see a kangaroo lying on its side in front of me. Its windswept brown coat is intact. I look around it for signs of scavengers, but I see none. It must have been hit recently. Over here, eagles and other birds of prey quickly do their job of eating the roadkill. Before resuming my run, I had to check one detail.

Kangaroo mothers carry their offspring in their pouch for many months, and that one happens to be a female. With the tip of my shoe, I gently probe the marsupial's belly. The reaction is immediate. A weak but perfectly audible breath escapes from her insides. What a scare it gives me! I wait for a vehicle to pass. A man finally stops and takes charge of the situation. I help him turn the animal on its back, and then the man plunges his hand into the ventral pouch and pulls out a newborn. He places it in my hands and then gets a blanket in his car. The joey breathes. Its skin is translucent, and I feel that its life is hanging by a thread. The man is heading towards Norseman, 400 kilometers away, where he will hopefully find a veterinarian. He takes the kangaroo from my hands and, seeing my emotion, reassures me with a laugh, "It's not like in your country here. Don't worry about kangaroos. We have millions of them!"

At the Cocklebiddy Roadhouse that day, I meet Bruce and Samantha, a couple of rescued eagles who are permanent residents of the place. They have been too injured to be released back into the wild and seem quite content in their enclosure, enjoying their celebrity status and posing for photos with tourists. The heavy birds need time to lift off from the road when they are busy cleaning roadkill, like my poor kangaroo, and as truck traffic can be fast, there are a lot of casualties. It's dangerous for wildlife to hang around the highway.

On days when we commute to a roadhouse for the night and back to my starting point the next morning, we have a system to ensure I restart exactly at the same spot. I tie a yellow, high vis hat up to a tree, pole, or road marker. The next morning, we drive until we spot the flashy yellow sign, so we don't have to rely on the precision of a satellite spot on our mobile phones. I pick up the hat and start the GPS again. A trick that works very well throughout the crossing.

After running the longest straight road in Australia (146 kilometers), crossing a forty-five-minute time zone, and plodding through a week of rain and cold temperatures (unusual in the Nullarbor), I make it to the Madura Pass on the Roe Plains. At this point, the road takes a sudden turn and plunges into a descent that takes me by surprise. I thought I was running at sea level but had been traveling on a low-altitude plateau. Now, I'm surrounded by noticeably denser, greener vegetation.

I realize that on both sides of the highway, the red sand has given way to a mixture of sandy earth and crushed shells. It takes me a bit of time to understand why, with the help of a Google search. I am running about thirty kilometers inland, parallel to the coast, and the ground I am running on was astonishingly the bed of the ocean, forty-five to fifteen million years ago. Around me are fossils as far as the eye can see. Once again, I feel like I'm treading on the floor of an open-air museum.

We cross into South Australia past Eucla, an old service town boasting the remnants of a telegraph station, an old jetty, and bleached-white whale bones dotted around. At long last, something to visit other than a roadhouse! The bracing smell of fresh air has replaced the earthy green fragrance of the plains. The landscapes are changing again. The dramatic cliffs of the Great Australian Bight, standing 100 meters tall, cut a very impressive figure to my right.

I run along the coast just as the southern whale breeding season begins. The whales come every year, between May and October, to the shallow, protected waters of the Australian Bight. Here, they can give birth safe from predators like great white sharks. James explores the coast on his bike, along the cliffs, during my run, scouting for observation points, and in the afternoon, he takes me to the best spots. We stay there, eyes on the bay below as the mammals float on the surface, breathe out formidable jets of water, or simply break through the surface to dive further away.

On approach to the mythical Nullarbor Roadhouse, I spot a dingo for the first time. I freeze in my tracks, a hundred meters from the animal, careful not to scare it. The dingo stares at me for a moment, then leaves the road belly down and ears folded back, with short strides, to get lost in the bush. I watch him for a long time, his sand-colored fur peeking out here and there as he moves away through the low vegetation. The dingo and I continue our course, leery of each other's presence. Tom sends me a message that evening after reading my daily blog report. During his world run in 2013, he ran into a dingo at the same spot. Could it be the same family, I wonder?

On the day we reach the last roadhouse of the crossing, a car pulling a large trailer slows down by my side as I am running. The man at the wheel offers me some muffins. He says he has seen me a few times over the past couple of weeks. I refrain from smiling and, seemingly unfazed, I answer, "You are Richard, right?'"

The look of surprise on his face is priceless! We had met a tandem-cycling couple a few days ago who told us about their encounter with a man named Richard who had taken it upon himself to clean the sideways of the Eyre Highway. He commutes in his car, pulling a large trailer where he keeps all the rubbish he collects, and sleeps in his car. He is a bit of a mysterious man and a sort of recluse. Before he drives off, he tells me he'll keep an eye out for me on the road.

A few days later, I am running on a small sidetrack parallel to the highway. On this lonely path, I see the silhouette of a man in the distance. He's dressed in black, standing still, and facing me.

My blood turns cold. I grab the phone from my side pocket and message James, "There's someone strange and scary on the trail. Maybe that could be the man who said he would be looking for me. I'm switching back to running on the highway. Meet me as soon as you can!"

As I proceed to cut through the vegetation towards the highway, I see the man in black taking the same route. "Damn!" I think it's looking bad. I make it to the road and see the man coming towards me at high speed on a bike. It's James! What a fool I am. He was not wearing his usual high-vis jacket and has given me a good scare! I blame myself and my poor vision for having thought that it could have been someone (maybe Richard) with ill intentions. The next day, we meet him again and take the time for a friendly chat at the end of my run. Richard is a nice man. Definitely an outsider, but certainly not a scary man at all!

My adventure across the Nullarbor is coming to an end. Its name means "treeless" in Latin, a misleading term since these plains are covered in scrub, bushes, greenery, and often eucalyptus, which I discovered there are several hundred different species. I have greatly enjoyed the crossing. I saw kangaroos, emus, wombats, dingoes, southern whales, eagles, and all kinds of parrots living in their natural environment. I appreciated every day in this desert, rich in wild and natural life and full of geological surprises, such as the blowholes. The only reason I'm looking forward to reaching Ceduna, the town that marks the end of the Nullarbor, boils down to one detail. I haven't changed my shoes since Valparaíso, and with almost 3,000 kilometers on the clock, I have holes in my soles!

I usually wear them out to the end. Since I land on the front of my foot, my stride is light, and my shoes, like my joints, are under much less pressure than those of the average runner. Despite this, after more than 2,500 kilometers, most shoes lose their stability, and the soles often puncture. I celebrate the end of the Nullarbor crossing with a new pair of shoes, the sixteenth of the odyssey. They will be the last. I only have 2,500 kilometers left until Sydney.

Ceduna is the first town we meet since leaving Norseman, and it makes for a welcome change of diet. Food quality throughout the Nullarbor depends strongly on each of the roadhouse's management teams. The Nundroo Roadhouse, manned by a couple of Indian Australians, served us delicious spicy curry. And I give the Madura establishment a five-star review for its exceptional lamb shanks, which we had three servings of. But aside from these two outstanding establishments, we have mostly been served microwaved food over the past month.

On a terrace overlooking the jetty, we sit down for dinner, watching the sunset in stunning bright yellow and orange stripes on the horizon. We indulge in the delicacy of local oysters, served with, of course, Australian white wine. We are toasting the new chapter of the crossing since James has now committed to continue by my side, "at least until Melbourne."

I can sense that he is torn between the need to get back to his house, his trees, his work, and the temptation to see this adventure through to the end, crossing together, the last continent of the journey. I am starting to think my "temporarily" retired stroller may never be used again. Meanwhile, it keeps its place in the motorhome.

25

OZ COUNTRYSIDE

The sheer size and wilderness of Australia is difficult to grasp for us Europeans. The continent covers an area larger than Europe but only has twenty-five million inhabitants concentrated in a few urban clusters. The cities of Perth, Adelaide, Melbourne, and Sydney alone are home to more than half of the country's population. This distant land is essentially unpopulated, apart from the centers of life located on its coasts.

The deserted Nullarbor Plains now behind me, I discover a world that is barely more urban (but certainly greener) and spackled with small country towns. I run through lush valleys and agricultural fields, pass by an abundance of livestock and vineyards the country is renowned for, and laugh along with the calls of the kookaburra.

I have two months of running left. The notion of time catches up and plays with me. The two and a half years I have spent on the road shake my thoughts, clashing with the reality of my slow progress. Is it another two long months? Or only two more months? With the finish line in sight, I am gripped by emotions that are as vivid as they are contradictory. There is a feeling that the adventure has just begun and a realization that its days are already numbered. I get lost in the immense and rich jumble of experiences it has offered me.

While running, I mentally scroll through the stages of the world run. I go through all the stages of the adventure, town by town, from Cabo da Roca to Istanbul, from Seattle to New York, from Maullín to Buenos Aires. I revel in this exercise, not only because it sharpens my memory, but because it conjures up sensations. Reliving the feeling of a sunrise, the weather that day, a pleasant encounter, watching animals, flora, or the landscape. During the course of a normal life, we do not remember precisely what we have felt every day over several years.

For my part, I have seven hundred days of travel engraved in my memory. No two runs are alike, the antithesis of the monotony and boredom many people wrongly imagine we suffer when running for so long. I try to stay in the present moment, to experience each stage until Sydney with the same intensity as the previous ones, and not let myself be overwhelmed by emotions.

Our nomadic life, tied to the motorhome, has become our comfort, a cozy nest, which is now a lot more than just a necessity, as was the case in the Nullarbor. We set camp every afternoon in a new holiday park. We plug in to get the heating going. We share a snack and a cup of tea and connect to the internet to do a bit of work. We get our token for the shower, where hot water is often distributed by tranches of five minutes straight. We go out for a stroll to visit the local sights. We cook our dinner on the communal barbecues, which we always find to be modern, clean, and spacious. Then we settle in when the sun goes down to watch a movie or read a book. We are at home with each other.

The Eyre Peninsula provides us with vast new experiences. On my way to Port Augusta, I have a wonderful day away from the highway on Caroona Road. With the Flinders Range in the background, I am accompanied for a while by bouncy kangaroos and a group of emus. I also spot, for the first time, the Sturt's Desert Pea: a bright red flower emblematic of South Australia, boasting scarlet, pea-shaped flowers adorned with a black bulbous center. Stunning, artsy, and precious.

At the end of a peaceful and contemplative rest day in Port Augusta, spent walking around the botanical gardens and skirting the Red Cliff overlooking the Spencer Gulf, James announces his decision to continue the journey to Sydney. I am relieved. We will experience the intense and highly charged emotions of crossing the finish line, side by side.

Meanwhile, I am set to reach Adelaide on July 14, and the consular network has invited me to join in the Bastille Day celebrations. The Honorary Consul of France, Marcia McLachlan, has organized my arrival. I meet her for a ceremony at the French Market, a food court selling heaps of European delicacies. We are then invited to dine at a fancy restaurant where all the dishes are paired with a different wine chosen, and presented by, Chester Osborn, a national celebrity and fourth-generation winemaker. He is quite an eccentric and charming character, sporting long, curly hair, wearing huge rings on each finger and dressed in a bright floral shirt with a wide collar straight out of the 1970s. At the end of the meal, he heads towards our table. We chat late while tasting the good wines of Chester, a little more than we should have. A memorable evening and a far cry from our quiet barbecues by the motorhome. It is also a foretaste of the gradual return to city life, to a certain worldliness.

The next day, we spend the afternoon at the Cleland Wildlife Park, where Australia's most famous native species roam freely in vast enclosures: Tasmanian devils, wombats, scores of kangaroos, and wallabies. We walk around and observe them in their environment, as if for the last time in the journey. Just before leaving, I am given the chance to approach a koala. I briefly bury my nose in its fur, which exudes the strong, sweet smell of eucalyptus. I catch a good whiff, eyes closed, recalling at once all the memories I have of the wildlife and nature of Western and Southern Australia.

Upon leaving Adelaide, I have two weeks of running ahead of me until Melbourne. The seasons being the opposite of what they are in Europe, it is the Australian winter that I feel now, and the temperatures cool down significantly as I move towards the southern polar circle. Once again, the landscapes change. I move away from the sea and the mountains, progressing inland. I don't meet many people. I run on country roads, dirt paths lined with eucalyptus, accompanied by the incessant cries of the sulphur-crested white cockatoos, who follow me for miles on end. I wonder if my presence is disrupting their habitat. Are they protecting their nests or just expressing their joy at seeing me among them? What a racket they make!

While I enjoy running to the sound of local wildlife, I'm looking forward to another kind of company upon reaching my next big stage, Melbourne. The French Consul, Myriam Boisbouvier, is a long-time friend of Pat Farmer, the man who famously ran around

Australia. A serious endurance runner, Pat also ran down America from its northernmost to its southernmost point.

Myriam has arranged the logistics, and I meet her husband, John, her son, Matthew, and Pat in the morning outside the western suburb of the megacity. The skyscrapers sticking up in the distance remain in sight as we head towards the Yarra River before entering the business district. The two friends are very chatty. I enjoy the conversation and banter, which makes for a very joyous and welcome change from the cockatoos! I listen as Pat tells me his stories, and I am fascinated by his longitudinal crossing of the Americas "from pole to pole." I enjoy his anecdotes, the story of his epic journey to the North Pole, and the frostbite from which he still has not recovered. Pat talks about some of his projects, and I notice that, like all the endurance adventurers I have met, he never stops. Would I, too, want to continue after this world run?

He asks me, and I realize that I don't have an answer. I sometimes think about what my life will be like once the adventure is over and how I will spend my days in the weeks and months that follow. I often discuss this with James, who has projects I look forward to participating in, like the restoration of a 1968 catamaran, for example. It's the same model as the one Rosie Swale-Pope (the only woman to have run around the world before me) traveled the oceans in as a pioneer. I plan for other adventures as if to protect myself from the inevitable emptiness that will follow the end of my journey. But as far as running is concerned, I don't have any particular ambitions at the moment. I can understand how this might seem strange coming from someone who runs her daily marathons with so much enthusiasm. Maybe I'm waiting to see a project take shape that will thrill me again, as much as the world run has.

In central Melbourne, we are joined by a few other runners. The weather is warm, and the terraces are full. It's a magnificent day with surprisingly springlike temperatures. Our small group finishes the run in front of the city hall, where a little reception awaits us, headed by Lord Mayor Sally Cap and Myriam. It seems this world run is getting some official recognition! I am met by a few students from the local French school, some veterans, and some representatives of the French community.

It is overwhelming to see the emotions brought about by the journey in the eyes of total strangers, especially in children. There is so much fascination associated with traveling around the globe. And doing it while running only amplifies the extraordinary nature of the odyssey. I promise to visit the school the next day, as they have prepared a general assembly in honor of the world run.

James and I then head off to the southern suburbs, where his friend Rosie is hosting us. What a delight to settle for a few days in a home after these long months spent sleeping in the motorhome. If my thoughts on the road are often articulated around the experience and memory of the run, these two days of rest in Melbourne, in a new environment, take my thoughts to another terrain.

A strange phenomenon occurs as I get closer to Sydney. Like Forrest Gump, who finishes his epic run accompanied by a crowd of supporters, I am no longer alone. I had set off solo on this journey with a very personal ambition to search for a unique and sensory experience of the world. I now feel a diffuse presence, a shared excitement in the welcome that I receive here in Australia, and the one that is being prepared by my friends in my hometown of Rouen. It is like a gradual, almost indescribable rising force. In the light of this distant but so real and warm presence, I begin to measure everything this trip has given me in return, far beyond what I had expected.

It has reconnected me to my roots, to my parents, my brothers, and my sister. We have lived together in this shared experience of almost three years, a real gift. It brought me closer to my friends, too. Those who joined this new adventure from the start, remaining faithful to my nomadic wanderings, and those who rallied around my journey. They have all wandered with me through my daily reports, and the ranks have thickened as I progressed. Bonds have tightened around this extraordinary journey.

It has also given me an anchor and traveling companion. A stranger at first, who joined me a few months ago, sharing the most beautiful chapter of my life and the most meaningful, too. James has crossed two continents by my side, and we have found, in this journey, the obvious foundation for a future together.

I look back at the lonely woman, stroller in hand, setting off from Cabo da Roca two and a half years ago with a mixture of tenderness and disbelief. What nerve! She dared to take the road with a small bag of belongings, a stroller, and the world in front of her. Yet, she lacked nothing because every day, the trip gave her precious experiences in return. Though my pockets are nearly empty as I approach the end of the journey, I am wealthier in a way that I only suspected could make me so much happier.

The rigors of this extreme nomadic life have equipped me with the essentials. How strange that without James' house burning down in the inferno of a Greek summer, he would not be a part of this adventure. He would not be with me. Both of us, living without material possessions, on the road, feeling complete and content in our journey of discovery. It is how, more determined than ever and in the wonderful company of family, friends, traveling and life companions, I set off towards Sydney.

The first day of running out of Melbourne is particularly grueling. Anne-Sophie, a member of the French alliance, runs by my side for twenty kilometers, then turns back, leaving me on my own again. That is when things start to turn south dramatically. I feel tired to an extent that is not comprehensible, especially as I have just had two full rest days. I have to sit down and take breaks, get up again, and a few kilometers later, lie down. I end up taking a nap on the side of the road. That is a first.

I end the run exhausted. James has been waiting for me in the van. He did not ride his bike today. He is also very tired and has flu-like symptoms. To top it all, he received a message from his friend Rosie, who hosted us for two nights. She has contracted the dreaded COVID-19. We buy two instant tests at the pharmacy, and the result is clear: we both test positive for the virus. Disaster! If there is a moment in this world run where I cannot afford to be late, it is for my arrival. And because it is planned for August 30, at the Opera House in three weeks exactly, there is simply no time to be sick.

26

SYDNEY, THE JOURNEY ENDS

Fortunately, the virus remains discreet. After the grueling day, I run my daily marathon without feeling any other symptoms. It complicates our logistics, though, as we are not allowed to be anywhere near people. While we wear a mask outside and stay in our motorhome as much as possible after the run is over, it is difficult to abide by all the rules of confinement when you live on the road. We still need to buy food and find a place to plug in our motorhome at night. But we do our best, cover our faces, keep our distance, and refrain from mingling.

I head northeast towards Sydney and feel the temperatures slowly rise. I cannot wait to join another family, the WRA. The WRA is a very exclusive club, made up of only six members to date, and is preparing to welcome me in as their seventh member. I receive a heartwarming call from Rosie, the only woman to have run around the world. She kindly wishes me well and congratulates me on my endeavor. I am touched and moved by her gesture. I am also going to meet its President, Phil Essam. Phil is a bit of a historian of long-distance running in Australia and a former ultra runner himself. He helped Jesper Olsen in his first run around the world and has met and encouraged every other world runner since then.

Using the trace of my satellite beacon, Phil finds me on the side of the Olympic Highway. I am overjoyed to see him. He has driven for hours to find me, and I give him a warm hug. We take time to stop and chat. I feel his emotions, too. I'm glad I didn't break my promise. When I shared my project with the WRA in 2019, I wrote to Phil, "We'll see each other in Sydney."

He officially welcomes me to the club, and while I appreciate his kindness and his words, I took them with a pinch of salt: there are still ten marathons left to run. I am not superstitious, but I have learned to welcome each day with the same humility. And maybe I don't want to jinx the whole thing by being over-confident. I tell Phil, "It's not over until it's over!"

Phil must have seen a fair amount of crazy people over the years embarking on the journey of a lifetime. Since I left, I have witnessed three of them start and give up after suffering an injury. It is an unforgiving journey and is a fine art to strike a balance that makes it sustainable. I think this partly explains Phil's enthusiasm. I didn't break my promise, nor did I give up, despite the global pandemic. I'm also a woman, the second only to join the ranks of the WRA. I resume my run with the wonderful feeling of already belonging to this family, and I cannot wait to meet my peers.

I await the last day with a mixture of impatience and disbelief. The adventure is coming to an end. Deep down, I don't want it to stop, and if it were up to me, I would continue on and on. But two years and eight months of complete self-financing have left my finances dry, and I don't have the means to continue any further. Not a penny left but a full heart and unique memories of the world. I also look forward to completing the journey, to savor a new feeling, that of having fulfilled the contract and achieved a phenomenal endurance performance.

At dawn on August 30, 2022, I meet Pat Farmer again in Moorebank, a western suburb of Sydney. After the run in Melbourne, he had promised to be by my side on the final stage of the journey. It is a hot day, and we start early to avoid the heat, taking as many breaks as needed. On the way, we meet James and his cousin, Mark, who lives in Sydney, riding their bikes. They film, take photos, and guide us through the suburban roads. Then, my friend Colin joins us at Petersham Park.

As we approach the city center, our little group slowly grows. A few French people from the Chamber of Commerce meet me at Pyrmont Bridge, along with members of the consulate and two local runners who heard about my route details on social networks. I am overwhelmed with intense sensations, an increased joy and satisfaction that energizes me even more than usual. It feels like I am being carried by my traveling companions just as much as by those in Europe who follow me from afar.

I enter the botanical gardens and finally catch a glimpse of the sea, an inlet of the South Pacific Ocean, to be precise. The lush and exotic alleys are beautiful, but I barely have time to appreciate their splendor. Everything seems to be moving so quickly now. At times, my breathing stops when the thought, "In a few strides, it's over," crosses my mind. Although I have often projected myself into the post-run period, I have never visualized my last strides specifically. I want to stop time.

But everything accelerates. A turn to the left, a turn to the right, and suddenly there it is. I see its unmistakable shape, the Sydney Opera House with its shiny white roof in the shape of sails billowing in the wind. I can feel my heart race, pounding hard in my chest. I'm smiling from ear to ear. The atmosphere is electric. I take out of my bag the large French flag that James had bought me and raise it aloft with both hands above my head, tears welling up in my eyes. I pass the gate that leads to the Opera House and stop running.

I bow to the assembly and switch off my GPS devices. That's it, it's over. I'm stunned. My thoughts freeze, and I drift through a strange cerebral void, a form of dissociation. The emotional shock is powerful. Mechanically, I rush towards the little crowd and hug my parents.

A few dozen people, waving small blue-white-red flags, welcome me with applause. They are members of the French community gathered by the consulate. I look around. I see some of my friends who now live in Sydney: Rosie, Stuart, and Phil, cyclists and former colleagues from Singapore, Vicky and Peter, friends from Greece.

All my predecessors finished their world run at home, surrounded by their loved ones and large crowds of thousands cheering them on. The vagaries of COVID-19 make me complete the adventure on the furthest possible continent, at the antipode of Rouen. It makes me feel all the more grateful for everyone who has made the trip to give me a perfect, unforgettable finish. The consulate offers me, in addition to a superb bouquet of native Australian flowers, an ultimate welcome.

On the steps of the country's most famous building, located on the edge of the Pacific Ocean, we gather under a bright blue sky and summery temperatures. I submit to the photos and selfies ritual one last time, receive congratulations, and share the joy of this unique and exceptional moment. Everyone is smiling. Gradually, I calm the flow of my emotions as the small crowd dissipates. After an hour, there is only a handful of us left.

At this moment, I distinguish in the distance, the silhouette of the man with whom I have corresponded with for almost five years. The one who told me, "You're ready," Tom Denniss. I am very moved to find myself face-to-face with him. Through his kindness and humble, normalizing attitude towards his journey, he has instilled in me, an ordinary woman, the confidence to launch into this extraordinary adventure, simply by encouraging me, listening, and letting me find my answers to live the adventure to the fullest.

Tom finished his world run in his homeland on September 13, 2013, at the Opera House in Sydney, almost nine years to the day before me. His last continental crossing was also Australia, and this year, he republished all his blog posts from his journey on Facebook. As we followed the same route from Perth to Sydney, his reports echoed my real-time experience and vice versa. I guess, in a way, my run must have brought back his memories. For me, it was as close as I could get to running in his footsteps.

After this short reunion, I spend the rest of the day with my parents. They have been by my side throughout, from my solo departure in Portugal to a Christmas in Seville, then Washington, DC, and New York, and now this festive arrival in Sydney. For them, too, today marks the end of a fabulous and shared adventure. My phone rings and vibrates all afternoon. It seems that the French media are finally interested in my story. I had sent a press release to a few media outlets without much expectation. At the end of each continental crossing, I had sent similar communications without generating any interest. This time, it is positive, and I am delighted that my completed journey captivates a few people.

The fact that I set a world record and a world first, may have something to do with it. Today, I become the only woman to have run across four continents. I also complete the fastest world run by a woman. The British runner, Rosie Swale-Pope, completed her epic journey in 2008, covering the land masses of the Northern Hemisphere (i.e., three continents). She took five years to return to her starting point. Her achievement was formidable, and she was a pioneer, running entirely self-supported throughout her journey. I do not doubt that my record of 28,249 kilometers in 825 days (697 days of running, 128 days of rest) will be broken without much difficulty—should another woman dare to take the plunge. In the meantime, it is mine!

In the afternoon, a beautiful video edited from segments filmed throughout the adventure and an interview recorded over the internet last night is posted on the Facebook page of a leading French paper. It goes viral on social networks, and I am amazed by the responses it generates. The various comments that are added continuously reflect the same feelings. My odyssey fascinates. Other videos follow, as well as some short reports for the national television news and a few articles in the written press.

I welcome with delight this small ray of light being shed on my journey. I have often been surprised that I did not manage to get any media interest throughout the effort. Neither the mainstream media nor specialized running magazines picked up on my story. On reflection, it was mostly my own doing. I think my twenty years of nomadism have something to do with it. I was from everywhere and nowhere. It showed in some of my choices.

I am French, but I didn't start my journey in France. I set off alone from Portugal without any fuss. I now finish the world run in Sydney, on the other side of the world. All other world runners had set off from their hometown, in their homeland, and that's where they'd finish. It creates a sense of expectation, where the return is awaited with awe and anticipation. A sort of hero's welcome.

I also wrote my website, daily blog, and social media posts in English, as opposed to my mother tongue. To top it all, I went by my nickname, Lootie, and not my full name. This added to the confusion about who I was and my nationality. The connection to my homeland, or any of my places of expatriation, was never quite established. Because of my nomadism, I was not part of any French community before the start, running or otherwise. All of this, I think, contributed to the absence of my presence in either the French press or on social media.

I rejoice, though from far away, at this sudden and short-lived burst of interest towards the world run. After all, it is a tribute to the extraordinary nature of this adventure. The journalists' questions oscillate between disbelief and admiration, and I only have a simple message to convey to them. You don't need to be a Wonder Woman or an extraordinary athlete to get there. You just need to have the desire and be carried by a curiosity about the world to triumph over any test.

We walk with my parents through the botanical gardens, which I remember seeing as I passed by at accelerated speed the day before. It is time to revisit the place, to appreciate the well-ordained beauty of nature, the exotic species, and the amazing views. We delight in the mischievous budgies, tamed and so unafraid of us. They land on our table to sip water directly out of our glasses. Then, we head over for dinner at James' cousin, Mark, and his wife Debbie's home. It makes for a peculiar and joyous moment, the first meeting between my family and that of James. Over a scrumptious dinner of delicacies and champagne, we share the joy of being together for this exceptional occasion.

The next day, James leaves early for the airport. The time has come for him to get back to his old life, away from the one exclusively focused on the world run for the past eight months. I pack my gear one last time and smarten up a bit. I get my hair cut and dress up to attend the consulate's invitation to the Tattersalls Club. It's a prestigious and heritage-listed historic club in Sydney, where we will celebrate the end of the journey. There are around fifty of us, friends, family, representatives of the French community, as well as Tom and a few of his friends. I take to the floor and have a large screen available to project some notable images from the world run.

I recount my trip in the past tense for the first time. I recall and share my most vivid memories, to give a measure of the vastness of the adventure. The dizzying run in Europe through the restrictions of COVID-19, the quest for freedom and discoveries that nothing could stop; the liberation represented by the crossing of the three other continents as they gradually opened up, the sensory experience of the world, the memory of everything I have seen, smelled, tasted, heard, and trodden with my feet; the lessons of history, civilization, geography, and geology that I picked up along the way; the people I have met and their generosity. Above all, the phenomenal emotion of having gone all the way, of having given it all, putting everything on the table to get there without concession. I push back tears as I tell this audience how much it was worth it, how I would leave again tomorrow if I could, and that the world is rich in lessons, surprises, and encounters. Freed from my fears, I have opened myself to the world, and it has left its mark on me forever.

I open it up to the audience for questions. As is often the case in this type of exercise, the number of shoes used seems to fascinate the guests! There were only sixteen. The shoes were all different since I bought what I found when the pair I wore fell apart. I am then asked about avoiding injury and what I attribute it to. I tell them about my body scan, listening to the body, and the absence of any artificial subterfuge.

I glance at Tom Denniss, present in the assembly, and we exchange a knowing smile. I had read it in his book. These were simple principles that he had put to the test. I followed in his footsteps, and we both completed the longest endurance journey in the world without any injury, and anecdotally, without as much as a blister. In a matter of hours, the festivities are over. I head back to the hotel with my parents.

Though I have allowed myself to celebrate the near end of the journey in Sydney, it is technically not over. The next day, September 1, 2022, I fly to Auckland, New Zealand, to complete my final run. The WRA requires that the runner pass by two antipodal points, and there are few such points in the world! Only 4 percent of the earth's surface has an antipodal point on land. Auckland happens to be one of these points, opposite the globe to Ronda, a place I ran through in Spain.

The five-kilometer run along the quays of Auckland is a very sobering end to the odyssey. Alone, without my companion, family or any supporters, I am with my thoughts, my head buzzing with excitement. The twenty-four hour plane ride back to Europe helps me land for good. Walking through the arrival terminal of Charles de Gaulle Airport with my small bag of belongings, I look around and wonder if others like me are coming back from such an extraordinary journey. Nobody can see the fireworks exploding in my heart.

EPILOGUE

This world run was not a fad. Neither a whim nor a midlife crisis nor a sudden desire to leave everything behind. It was a continuation of the nomadic life that I had led for more than twenty years in a lifelong quest to see the world. Before setting off alone on the roads, I had rid myself of the fear of the unknown, fear of others, fear of the leaps of faith.

These twenty years of globetrotting had cemented my motivation and determination to experience the world. The question never arose to seek out reasons for my commitment. They were obvious, anchored in me, and were never shaken by the difficulties I faced. Not once during this trip, whatever the conditions or the obstacles, did I say to myself that I would have preferred to be elsewhere or do something else.

I owe to my nomadism the three key ingredients of my success. Freedom from fears, the evidence of my commitment, and the long-standing emancipation from the supposed limits of my condition as a woman. My doubts, questions, and curiosity about the world are not the prerogative of men or women specifically. We all carry them within us. The idea never crossed my mind that I was less suited than a man to partake in any adventure, professional or otherwise.

With this world run, I also contribute to placing more women in the sphere of adventurers. I am only the second woman to have accomplished a run around the world. And the fastest, though truly, this doesn't mean much to me. I am the first woman to have crossed four continents, running from ocean to ocean. All this is ratified and validated by an independent authority, the WRA. I wish this would inspire more women and empower others to take the challenge and launch on their own beautiful adventures or life dreams.

This book is the ultimate gift of this world run. I couldn't have imagined a more beautiful way to end my journey than with these long months devoted to writing. Because the shock of the end is brutal.

The body adapts to its daily marathons, endorphins, dopamine, adrenaline, and serotonin; the cocktail of natural drugs produced during exercise. But much more than the running, what I missed when the adventure ended was the dizzying intensity with which I experienced each day of this world run. Every day a new journey, a new sunrise over a new landscape, a new stopover village, new encounters, a new sensory experience, new lessons, and discoveries. And every day, the satisfaction, the joy of progressing on an extraordinary adventure, outside of time, outside of conventions, an adventure that evokes a universal dream that captivates. A journey that made me escape the dictatorship of time and deadlines, feeling lucky to live my life to the fullest, and demonstrate every day my enthusiasm for this world that I spend my life traveling through.

The essence of the journey I have been through has been perfectly encapsulated in the poem "Ithaka" by the Greek poet Constantine Cavafy.

> "As you set out for Ithaka
> hope your road is a long one,
> full of adventure, full of discovery."

It is an ode to the voyage that Ulysses undertook back to his homeland. An invitation for the traveler to set out on a long road full of discoveries and adventures, but it's also a warning. Fear is sterile, and you only meet the objects of your fear when you carry them within you. It's an encouragement for Ulysses to rejoice in the daily discoveries, learn from his encounters, and let his senses feel the world. In the final strophes, which are so much in my mind as I conclude this journey and this book, Cavafy lays it out. When you arrive, there is nothing else to expect of Ithaka. The destination has given the traveler everything by putting him/her on the road, and through this, they have garnered experience, knowledge, and maturity.

The poem alludes to life as a journey, one that is universal and touches us all. This is why it resonates so much with all the people I have met, and why it is so important to share the story.

I like to think of the world run as another stage in my life journey. A stage that started in Marathon, took me around the world and ended with me living on a Greek island, not far from the real-life Ithaka. I haven't reached my Ithaka yet. My thirst for my syrup of the world is not yet quenched. The desire for elsewhere, for discovery, is still burning in me. It is the journey that's important, not the destination. I keep Ithaka in my sights, but far, far ahead …

MY WORLD RUN IN NUMBERS

FOR A FULL ACCOUNT OF THE JOURNEY,
WITH ALL MY DAILY BLOG POSTS AND PICTURES,
PLEASE VISIT: WWW.LOOTIE-RUN.COM

- 28,249 kilometers run
- 697 running days
- 128 rest days (1 per week)
- 40.5 kilometers average per running day
- 9.2 kilometers-per-hour average speed
- 4 continents crossed from west to east (Europe, North America, South America, Oceania)
- 16 pairs of shoes
- Zero injuries
- World record for the fastest run around the world (woman)
- First woman to have run across 4 continents

ACKNOWLEDGMENTS

My parents, Brigitte and Pierre, my siblings and spouses, Florence and Wilfried, Matthieu and Anne, and Antoine. My nephews and nieces, Clément, Milo, Camille, Félix, Alice, Gaspard.

My friends: Stéphanie and Xavier Heyte, Laurence and Yves Tomballe, Dimitris and Vicky Moraitis, Lisa Marston and Peter Miller, Elias Rokas, David and Miranda Lavery, Sylvain and Yael Virey, Céline and Chris Petersen, Fanny and Stéphane Bodin, Sharon Silverwood-Robson, Annick Masselot, Colin and Odette McDonald, Kostas and Alex Sapounakis, Caroline Vimont, Erwan Philippe, Jérome and Finn Rasse, Alain and Isa Crottaz, Luisa and Stan de Livonniere, Stephane and Ioanna Wagner, Catherine and Joe Zaccaria, Christelle Giraud-Nydegger, Seng and Justyna Chan, Marc and Maria Sundberg, Elodie Gardies, Donald and Moraig Bain, Rosie and Stuart Oldham, Vicky and Peter Aloupi, Debbie and Mark Ainsworth, Rosie Lugg, John Cowden, and Jim Rowe.

The diplomatic network: Olivier and Sayeh Gauvin in Istanbul, Ariane Ogier in Seattle, Yannick Tagand in Chicago, Jeremie Robert in New York, Claudia Scherer-Effosse in Buenos Aires, Marcia McLachlan in Adelaide, Myriam and John Boisbouvier-Wylie in Melbourne, and Anne Boillon in Sydney.

The International French Schools of Singapore, Istanbul, Chicago, and Buenos Aires.

My peers: Jesper Olsen, Rosie Swale-Pope, Tom Denniss, Tony Mangan, Kevin Carr, and Serge Girard.

Women for Women International: Laurie Adams, Lauren DiSilvio, and Ramone Segree.

Some of the amazing people I met along the way: Lisa Stranc-Bliss, Pat Farmer, Fergus Owen, Alexis Hanquinquant, Connie Karras, Phil Essam, Jan and Gerald Wieler, Victoria and Franklin Wassmer, Margarita Panagopoulou, Georgia Mitsou, Lindita Xikia, Christos Karagiannidis, Panagiotis Theofilas, Petros Parthenis, Giorgos Kanakis, Loukas Patrilas, Kostas Palantzas, Antoine Poupinel, Etienne Colin, Valentin Schwertz, Jeremy Stassin, Valentin Comps, Raymonde and Christian Detry, Beatrice Reininger, Marianne Ferre, Stephane Flueli, Urs Nietlispach, Gunhild Swanson, Greg Wallweber, Chris Morlan, Jo Schubring, Aric Trantum, Mindy Graeth, Herman Schreven, Angela Wells, Crystal Backman, Jacob Pittman, David Pitrich, Ivan Perez Munoz, and Fabio Morales.